D0099956

THE COOKING OF SINGAPORE

THE COOKING OF SINGAPORE

Great Dishes from Asia's Culinary Crossroads

by
Chris Yeo
and
Joyce Jue

Photography by
Keith Ovregaard

An Astolat Book
HARLOW & RATNER
Emeryville, California

Food Styling: Susan Massey-Weil
Prop Styling/Backgrounds: Debbie Dicker
Jacket Design: The Design Office of Wong & Yeo
Illustrations: Pauline Phung
Typography: Classic Typography
Production: Schuettge & Carleton

Props for photography:
Cedanna, San Francisco, pg. 12, 63
R.H., San Francisco, pg. 73
Shiki, San Francisco, pg. 88

Library of Congress Cataloging-in-Publication Data

Yeo, Chris, 1953–
The cooking of Singapore : great dishes from Asia's culinary crossroads / by Chris Yeo and Joyce Jue ; photography by Keith Ovregaard.
p. cm.
"An Astolat book."
Includes index.
ISBN 0-9627345-6-X : $24.95
1. Cookery, Singapore. I. Jue, Joyce, 1947– . II. Title.
TX724.5.S55Y46 1993
641.595957–dc20 92-40615
CIP

Printed in Singapore

10 9 8 7 6 5 4 3 2 1

Harlow & Ratner
5749 Landregan Street
Emeryville, CA 94608

For Kelly, Julian, and Andrew
C.Y.

For Randy
J.J.

ACKNOWLEDGEMENTS

I would like to thank the following people for helping make this book possible:

My sweet and loving wife, Kelly, and my sons Julian and Andrew, for their love, strength, and many sacrifices over the years.

Mum & Dad, for all their help and encouragement in starting Straits Cafe.

My brothers and sisters, especially Joseph who was there at the very beginning of Straits Cafe, my mother-in-law, my father-in-law, my brothers-in-law and sisters-in-law, and my whole extended family for their support and assistance—I couldn't begin to count the ways they have all helped.

My dear friend and mentor, Joyce Jue, and my publishers and editors, Elaine Ratner and Jay Harlow, for giving me the insight to believe in myself and in this book.

My wonderful Nonya cook, Jenny Fong, who has taught me so much, as well as the other excellent chefs I have been fortunate to work with at Straits Cafe.

—C.Y.

Ten years ago my husband introduced me to a business associate, Jonathan Read, and his wife, Eve Lam, who were visiting from Singapore. We often talked about the great foods of Asia and of their particular fondness for the Nonya cooking of Singapore. Checking my hearing, I asked "What kind of cooking?" They seemed stunned by my ignorance, and matters only worsened when I drew a blank on the phrase "Straits Chinese." My questioning has continued to this very day, leading to my personal discovery of a fabulous cuisine and fascinating culture and history, and to this book.

Shortly after, the Reads' enthusiasm took me to Singapore to have a first-hand look and sampling of Nonya cuisine. Jon also insisted that I visit the Malaysian cities of Kuala Lumpur and Malacca, the latter one of the largest settlements of Straits Chinese. I tasted food in 4-star hotels and street hawker stalls and even pulled off the road to a roadside durian stand.

They gave me Terry Tan's *Straits Chinese CookBook* and other literature about the Straits Chinese. It was the tip of the iceberg of a new cuisine, at least for me. I have them to thank for this delicious and intriguing introduction.

A few months later, I returned with my husband to Kuala Lumpur and met Mr. Yap Lim Sen. Another great gastronome, he insisted on sharing his love of Nonya cooking with me as well. During a business meeting with my husband, he had his driver take me to a Kuala Lumpur hotel for what he considered the best steamed pomfret in town. Like many of the hotel restaurants in Asia, it was outstanding. The next day he flew us to Penang, the other large Straits settlement in Malaysia. I still remember savoring the marvelous breakfast noodles we had in an open-air hole-in-the-wall street cafe.

Back home I researched all my cookbooks and found only three paragraphs and not one recipe on Nonya cooking (in the Time-Life book *Pacific and Southeast Asian Cooking*). I felt

I had discovered a new cuisine (at least new to Westerners). I was hungry for knowledge and recipes, and to taste more. Each time I returned to Asia I sought out more recipes and more information on this cuisine.

Then one day as I drove down Geary Boulevard in San Francisco, my eyes caught a subtle teal green, pale blue, and pink awning advertising the Straits Cafe. We walked in and, with optimism, ate. Our dream had come true—San Francisco finally had a Singaporean restaurant.

I owe a great deal of gratitude to Chris Yeo, his lovely wife, Kelly, and their chef, Jenny Fong. I appreciate their allowing me into their kitchen to learn, test, and sample, and basically mess up their schedule. After days, weeks, and months spent in the Straits Cafe kitchen with Chris and Jenny I came to understand the nuances and the characteristics of Singaporean cooking. But equally fascinating and pleasurable was to partake in the social interaction of the multicultural heritage of Singaporeans. I listened with amazement as Chris and Jenny switched back and forth in mid-sentence among three dialects of Chinese, Malay, and English in their dealings with the cooks. Being there made me feel like a part of their family.

I am profoundly thankful to Elaine Ratner and Jay Harlow for giving me the opportunity to write this book for the American cook. Skeptical at first of the idea of a whole book devoted to this little-known cuisine, they kept their minds and palates open. Their first tastes of Chris's food removed any doubts, and *The Cooking of Singapore* was born.

I also want to thank the photographic team that has now helped me produce three beautifully photographed cookbooks. It is always a pleasure working with photographer Keith Ovregaard and stylists Debbie Dicker and Susan Massey-Weil. My appreciation goes also to illustrator Pauline Phung.

The unsung hero in the team effort of producing a cookbook is my husband, Randy. He tasted it all, the good and the bad, and stood behind me through the best and the worst parts of producing a book.

—J.J.

CONTENTS

INTRODUCTION

I grew up in a large family in Singapore. I attended hotel and catering school there, then went to London, England to study hair design. In 1979, I moved to San Francisco and opened a hair salon in the Haight-Ashbury district.

Although the salon was very successful, I kept going back to one of my earlier dreams, which was to open a restaurant. Soon after moving to San Francisco I realized that in this world-class restaurant city there was no Singaporean restaurant. The longer I stayed away from Singapore, the stronger grew my nostalgic longing for the wonderful, flavorful cooking of my childhood. Depending on memory and some very imprecise old recipes, I began experimenting, trying to recreate the many exotic flavors of Singapore using a combination of imported and California ingredients.

In 1987 I was able to realize my dream. I opened the Straits Cafe, named after the Straits Chinese settlements which were among the first communities in what is now known as Singapore. My mother came from Singapore to help me develop the menu and to ensure the authenticity of the food. Since then we have had a series of talented chefs, each of whom contributed his or her own special skills.

In the interest of further spreading the word about what I (and many others) consider one of the world's great cuisines, I am happy to share with you some of the Singaporean recipes we have so lovingly and painstakingly recreated at the Straits Cafe.

Chris Yeo
San Francisco, 1993

The first time I went to the Straits Cafe in San Francisco, I was greeted and shown to my table by its exuberant chef-owner, Chris Yeo. I was immediately struck by his youthful energy and by the restaurant's modest yet chic decor.

Without being stereotypic, the Straits Cafe conveys the authentic spirit of Singapore. Wooden shutter doors hanging from the high walls remind me of the old-fashioned two-story shophouse architecture common throughout Asia and old Singapore. Jutting out from the shutters are clothes-line poles "decorated" with children's T-shirts and trousers, also reminiscent of Asia. On the high ceilings, fans with long blades agitate *faux* palm trees, cooling the air and circulating cooking aromas from the kitchen. Chris cleverly designed the palm trees from burlap bags, twisting them around the building's support posts to create the trunks, then adding large palm fronds at the top.

The omnipresent, elusive aromas escaping from the kitchen to tease my nose and flirt with my appetite reassured me on that first visit that I was soon to enjoy again the unforgettable, gutsy food I had loved in Singapore. I sat down and surveyed the menu. It offered many of the traditional dishes of Malaysia, Indonesia, India, and China. Undecided because of the immense variety and the mix of ethnic cuisines to choose from, I weakened. I ordered it all—one of the lunch noodle dishes, a few appetizers, a dinner entree, soup, and a main course salad. In one seating, at one meal, I enjoyed four different ethnic cooking styles, just like I do when I am in Singapore. They tasted like they do in Singapore, and their presentation echoed the charming, provincial, yet ultra-modern elegance of that country. Here, in San Francisco, was the very essence of Singapore—a fusion of East and West, of old and new, of tradition and contemporary sophistication.

I knew that I had to get to know this multi-talented Singaporean man, the ingenious decorator and cook who had had the courage and determination to introduce his native food to the U.S. by opening an authentic Singaporean restaurant in San Francisco.

This cookbook is a collection of Chris Yeo's recipes from the Straits Cafe. It is also a book about Singapore, its many diverse nationalities, its wealth of exciting food, and its intriguing food history. To me Singaporean cooking, as it is practiced in Singapore and in San Francisco, is one of the most lively and appealing cuisines in the world.

Joyce Jue
San Francisco, 1993

ONE ISLAND, FOUR CUISINES

SINGAPORE'S CULINARY POSITION IN ASIA AND THE WORLD

Modern Singapore is a nation just over a quarter of a century old, with a multi-cultural population made up of so many groups it is difficult to identify an indigenous style of cooking. With the exception of the cooking of highly trained imperial-style Chinese chefs who immigrated to Singapore from Hong Kong, the country has no *haute cuisine* like that developed for royalty in Thailand. The cooking of Singapore is defined by an abundance of ethnic dishes of humble origins.

In Singapore the same popular home-style country dishes are served by outdoor street vendors, in covered "food centers" (sanitized versions of hawker centers), and in plush and opulent restaurants. As in America, it is quite in vogue for fine restaurants to take basic home-style dishes and give them a "face-lift." Contemporary Singaporean cooks have preserved many traditional dishes and have resurrected some that were nearly extinct, often adding a new sophisticated look and serving them in new settings. In recent years Singaporean cooking has become a major player in the international culinary arena. Its arresting aromas, intriguing ingredients, striking flavors, and colorful presentations have seduced gastronomes from around the world and made a considerable impression on the international culinary community.

WHAT IS SINGAPOREAN COOKING?

There is a great deal of confusion among Westerners as to what Singaporean cuisine actually is and whether it is indigenous. Unlike most nations where there is one native cuisine, Singapore has four major styles of cooking that could be considered indigenous. In this way Singaporean cooking is like American. America is a multi-cultural nation with cooking traditions that reflect many immigrant cultures—European, Hispanic, Asian, African, and Middle Eastern. Singaporean cooking is an amalgamation of four distinct kitchens representing three nationalities (Chinese, Malay-Indonesian, and Indian) and a unique sub-culture officially referred to as Peranakan but affectionately called Nonya or Straits Chinese by the locals. The Nonya cooking style, which grew out of the marriage of Chinese men to Malay women, is the most intriguing in Singapore. Until the recent efforts to preserve it, it had almost become extinct.

When Sir Stamford Raffles declared Singapore a free-trading post in 1819, Malays, southern Chinese, Tamils from southern India, and a sprinkling of Europeans, Armenians, and Arabs settled in Singapore, turning it from an isolated jungle-like island into a sprawling, cosmopolitan, international banking center. Each group brought along its traditional foods. Adopted immigrant dishes such as Hainanese Chicken Rice, Peranakan *Laksa,* Teochew *Chow Kway Teo* and *Chap*

Chye, Malay-Indonesian Beef *Rendang* and *Satay,* and Indian *Roti Prata* have become known as Singapore's "national dishes." They underscore the variety of ethnic cultures and nationalities that make up Singapore in the same way that such "American" standbys as hot dogs, pizza, spaghetti and meatballs, tacos, and today's popular focaccia, mu shu pork, roasted eggplant, and lavash sandwiches reflect the American melting pot.

As a broad generalization, it is safe to say that Chinese, Malay-Indonesian, Indian, and Nonya cooking together represent Singapore's national cuisine. It is still possible to find these four cooking styles in their purely traditional forms in spite of the pressures of modernization. At the same time, the four styles have also integrated, borrowing and sharing ingredients, techniques, and ideas, and have gradually evolved hybrid dishes that can be found only in Singapore.

In addition to the basic four, other cooking styles also thrive. During Singapore's formative years, East met West and created a local form of "Eurasian" cooking. Born from primarily Portuguese-Asian intermarriages, this exotic East-West style is unlike the western concept of East-West cooking. It is found in Portuguese-Eurasian homes but not in restaurants.

Singapore is also where East meets East, inspiring extraordinary "Pan-Asiatic" flavors. In the near future, culinary inspirations resulting from the continuous crossover of diverse ethnic Asian cultures may give birth to a truly native Singaporean cuisine. Although there are those who argue that Peranakan cooking is the national cuisine of Singapore, the only really definitive thing that can be said about Singaporean cooking today is that it is just now blossoming and is still very much a cuisine in the making.

DINING IN SINGAPORE

Home cooking is universally accepted as the best food in Singapore. If at all possible, the best way to sample local foods is in a home. A popular alternative, as throughout Asia, is to dine in the outdoor hawker centers where home-style dishes are the attraction.

Although hawker food stalls are throwbacks to the past, no Singaporean would ever think of giving them up. Setting up a food stall has always been a way for new immigrants to start their own business with little capital. Most hawkers are mom and pop enterprises in which the mother and father cook and run the business and the children are expected to serve. The food is mostly one-dish meals, eaten on the run or as snacks at any time of day. The hawker centers are outdoors, typically in spaces that are parking lots during the day. At dusk, the hawkers wheel in their mobile kitchen carts, set up portable outdoor tables and stools, and suspend strings of naked light bulbs. Each stall serves just a few dishes; the best often serve just one. To order food, customers need only point to a display dish. Moments later the food, cooked on the spot, is brought to your table.

Food courts are newer, more upscale, air-conditioned versions of the hawker centers, set up under a government-initiated project to create a more sanitary eating environment. Primarily serving Malay, Chinese, or Indian one-dish meals different from restaurant fare, they are popular for casual lunches in a comfortable environment.

Hawker-style food is also available in tired and worn old-fashioned shophouse cafes and coffee houses. These are typically open storefront shops that serve both hawker food and a range of restaurant fare on utilitarian tables. The rooms are decor-less and mundane, with fluorescent lighting against white tile walls. Customers come for the food, not the ambiance, and it is well worth it.

In addition, every respectable Singaporean hotel serves authentic local fare in its coffee shop or restaurant. Singaporeans expect it, and the hotels depend on local patronage as much as on hotel guests. Many food aficionados contend that the food is better at the hawker stalls, yet daily full houses at the hotel coffee shops attest to their popularity.

For special occasions, banquets are a favorite means of entertaining and celebration in Singapore, whether it's a wedding, a "red egg" baby party, or one of the exhausting number of ethnic festivals. The Chinese banquet food in Singaporean hotels and restaurants ranks as high as in other major cosmopolitan cities. Malay cooking, although relatively simple and provincial, has been updated and refined. A growing number of fancy Malay restaurants, as well as restaurants serving Indian, Nonya, and the other ethnic cuisines, are popping up throughout Singapore.

HISTORICAL ROOTS

Singapore's location makes it a natural crossroads. The island nation is situated just off the southern tip of the Malay peninsula—a point at which the South China Sea and the Java Sea meet the Malacca Strait, the main sea route connecting the Pacific and Indian oceans. To the west, south, and east lie the Indonesian islands of Sumatra, Java, and Borneo, and to the north lies the Gulf of Thailand, which borders Thailand, Cambodia, and Vietnam. Geographically, Singapore is a major hub of international commerce; gastronomically, it is the culinary bazaar of the East.

From the 5th to the 13th century, Singapore was known as Temasek or "sea town" and was part of an intricate network of small Southeast Asian trading centers. In the 13th century, while part of the Javanese Majapahit empire, it was given its current name, Singa Pura—the "Lion City." In the 15th century, during political upheaval and a power struggle between the Javanese and Siamese powers, Singa Pura was destroyed and it literally reverted to its natural jungle state. For the next 400 years it was inhabited only by small communities of Malay fishermen.

As the wild jungle grew, Dutch, Portuguese, English, and French traders sailed by, keeping an eye on the desolate island. Early in the 19th century, as a result of deals among the Dutch, English, and local leaders, Singapore came under the administration of the British East India Company headquartered in India. Thomas Stamford Raffles, a young merchant working for the

East India Company, saw in the tiny island the potential for a prosperous trading port. He arrived in 1819 and promoted the city's growth as a center for free trade to rival the Dutch ports of Indonesia. He helped design the city, implemented a plan for its government, and founded its legal and educational institutions. He established (and designed) Singapore's Botanical Gardens and, with the help of its director, began what would develop into a highly successful rubber industry on the Malay Peninsula.

As a thriving port city, Singapore was a magnet for traders and settlers. Southern Chinese traders as well as laborers attracted by rubber plantations and tin mines soon joined the original Malay fishermen and farmers. Settlers from the nearby Indonesian islands and Tamils from southern India, brought as indentured laborers for the rubber industry, all sought the opportunities provided by the new city. An 1824 census reported a population of 10,000, including 45% Malay, 30% Chinese, 17% Buginese (from Celebes, Indonesia), and 7% Indian, with the remainder Europeans and Arabs. By 1850 the population would grow to 60,000, including 53% Chinese, 23% Malay, 14% Indian, 7% Buginese, and 3% Arab and European.

Each group brought its native cuisine and ingredients with it to Singapore. Different ethnic groups, and even different dialect groups, were kept in separate residential districts by British decree, a divide-and-rule measure intended to avert any desire to unify and rebel. As a result, each group preserved its culture and traditions, and continued cooking in the style of its native country.

In 1826 the British made Singapore the governing center for the Straits Settlements, which included Penang, Malacca, and Singapore. In 1867 the Straits Settlements became a Crown Colony. The British continued to control Singapore until it fell to the Japanese in World War II. At the end of the war in 1945 it was returned to British rule. In 1946 British rule of the Straits Settlements ended; Singapore became a separate Crown Colony, and Penang and Malacca became part of the Federation of Malaya, a British protectorate. In 1959 the British granted Singapore self-rule, and Lee Kuan Yew, a young, energetic, British-educated Singaporean, was elected its first Prime Minister. Lee Kuan Yew created the Singapore we know today—one of Asia's most prosperous and cosmopolitan international banking and financial cities. In 1963 Singapore joined the new nation of Malaysia; two years later it separated from Malaysia and established itself as an independent republic.

Today Singapore's population of 2.5 million is primarily Chinese from Fujian (the Hokkien) and Guangdong (the Cantonese and Teochew) provinces. They constitute 76% of the population; the rest is Malay (15%), Indian and Pakistani (7%), and 2% other races. A rich and diverse assortment of cooking styles continues to co-exist, each in its purest form, without compromise. Only in Singapore can one dine in local food centers and enjoy, side by side, the authentic dishes of a multitude of ethnic regions.

Even as they preserved their diversity, over time the cultures of Singapore began to assimilate and integrate with each other, forming some very novel culinary marriages. The crossover of techniques, ingredients, and seasonings from Chinese, Malay, Indian, and Nonya traditions established a new style of cooking found only in Singapore.

THE SINGAPOREAN CHINESE COOK

During the early 1800s, a large number of Chinese immigrated to Singapore. They came from Malacca (a port on the west coast of Malaysia), the island of Penang, and (to escape famine, civil war, and poverty) southern China. The southern Chinese included Cantonese from Guangdong, Hokkien from Amoy and the surrounding countryside in southern Fujian, Teochew from near the seaport of Swatow at the border of Guangdong and Fujian provinces, and Hailam from the island of Hainan.

The settlers arrived loaded down with woks, cleavers, steamers, and clay pots. They brought their essential seasonings—soy sauce, ginger, garlic, green onions, peanut and sesame oil, and preserved soybean cooking condiments—plus dried black mushrooms, lily buds, and bean curd in all its various forms. Just the basics. In their separate enclaves (separated by dialect) they continued to prepare their pork, chicken, duck, and seafood as they always had, with crisp vegetables and appropriate seasonings and sauces.

The Chinese clung to their traditional techniques of stir-frying, deep-frying, braising, steaming, and poaching. They emphasized the importance of fresh ingredients and the concept of balancing texture, taste, and color. Cantonese *dim sum* specialties and the high art of banquet food, the *haute cuisine* of China, became very much a part of Singapore's cooking.

THE MALAY-INDONESIAN COOK

The Malay-Indonesian cook is also a major player in the culinary history of Singapore. Through time the distinguishing characteristics of Malay and Indonesian cooking have blurred. Given their geographic proximity, and the fact that they are related linguistically and ethnically, it is not surprising the two cultures share the same spices, seasonings, and ingredients. As a result of migration between the islands of Sumatra, Java, and Borneo and the various Malay states, intermarriage, and cultural assimilation, the foods of the two countries mingled. In Singapore today the two styles of cooking are difficult to differentiate.

Traditional Malay cooking was greatly influenced by visiting traders from India, China, and the Middle East. Malay cooks readily adopted spices, herbs, and seasonings introduced by the traders, as well as their cooking techniques.

These they added to their own lavish array of colorful and rich local seasonings. Such indigenous floral plants as *daun serai* (lemongrass), *daun kesom* (polygonum), *daun pandan* (pandan leaf), *daun limau perut* (kaffir lime leaf), and *daun kari* (curry leaf) accent their food with seductive perfumy highlights. Malay food also exudes the delicious herbaceous bouquet of such rhizomes as *lengkuas* (also known as *galangal* or *kha,* its Thai name), *kunyit* (turmeric), and ginger. Inspired by local Indians, Malaysian cooks in Singapore further punctuate their food with the dried seeds of fennel, cumin, coriander, cardamom, and cloves.

Shallots, garlic, lemongrass, lengkuas, and chiles are among the "wet" ingredients of the *rempah,* or spice blend, that flavors Malay-style curries (see Learn To Make Rempah, page 24). *Buah keras* (candlenut), a hard, oily nut once used to make candles, is added to the rempah to enrich and thicken the curries.

The Malays have a fondness for tamarind. It lends a unique sweet and citrus-like sour taste to *sambals, gulais* (curries), and sauces. They accent their sauces with *blachan,* an enigmatic fermented shrimp paste; one tiny dab of roasted *blachan* penetrates to the soul of a dish, imparting a gutsy taste that defines Malaysian cooking. Coconut milk, widely used throughout Southeast Asia, mellows the spiciness of chiles and marries the flavors of dried ground spices in the Malay kitchen. All of these ingredients contribute to the hearty, spicy, fragrant, and earthy character of both Malay and Indonesian cooking.

The Malays are mostly Muslim; therefore, pork is forbidden. They grill mutton, beef, fish, shellfish, and chicken whole or cut into thin strips of *satay.* They dip the meat into a spicy-sweet peanut sauce or turn it into luscious curries served with *nasi* (rice). The Malay meal at home is quite simple. Some rice, a main course of fish or poultry or both, vegetables, and a *sambal,* a table condiment which may be hot and spicy, sweet, or chutney-like, make up a typical menu. Malay cooks "wash" their fish in tamarind liquid to rid it of any fishy smells, then fry it in oil, or rub or stuff it with a *rempah* (spice blend) then wrap it in a banana leaf and grill it. They sometimes cook fish in a *gulai* (curry), or braise it with a sour hot sauce, or simply grill it naked. The majority of Malay foods are *goreng* (fried or deep-fried), simmered into a *gulai,* or *panggang* (grilled or barbecued).

THE INDIAN COOK

The majority of Indians in Singapore are Tamils from Madras and Kerala in southwest India. Their contributions to Singaporean cuisine include such dishes as *mee goreng,* a distinctive version of Indonesian-style fried noodles, and Indian-style *rojak,* a spicy salad originally from Java.

A wonderful array of Indian breads has become part of Singapore's lifestyle. It's hard to pass up an Indian breakfast of *roti prata,* a griddle-fried flaky white-flour bread served with a thin curry sauce. Other typical breakfast breads are a thin, slightly sour-tasting pancake called *dosay* and *idli,* a steamed bun made with a black-skinned lentil and rice flour batter. Equally tempting for a snack or lunch is *murtabak,* a griddle-fried *roti* (Indian bread) stuffed with spiced minced mutton or beef, eggs, and onions.

"Curry" transcends every cultural barrier. The idea of "curry" is one of the great contributions of the Indian kitchen to the international culinary world. Here in the West one curry powder blend is considered convenient and satisfactory for most dishes; not so in Singapore. Indian cooks have shared the secrets of working with spices with all their Singaporean neighbors. The average Singaporean of any race knows that cardamom and cloves work well with meats but overpower vegetable dishes, and that formulations for the various *garam masala* mixtures contain four to six or more ground spices. Black pepper, coriander, and cumin form the base of the spice mix; turmeric, cloves, and cardamom may be included.

Malay, Chinese, and Nonya cooks in Singapore have all embraced Indian spices and methods. In Singapore there are spice shops whose merchants' sole job is to formulate blends of spices to a cook's specifications for particular dishes.

Many agree that some of the best Indian cooking in the world is found in Singapore. Southern Indian may be the original style of Indian cooking in Singapore, but the northern style, less hot but spicier, is also represented. Indian vegetarian cooking, too, has greatly influenced the cooks of Singapore.

THE NONYA COOK

The mixing of cultures in Singapore has produced a number of exciting blends of cooking styles. The most notable from a culinary standpoint is Nonya cooking, a style that has broken ground in establishing a culinary identity for Singapore. As recently as ten or twenty years ago, this unique blend was on the edge of extinction. Today, there is a resurgence of interest in Nonya cooking among the Peranakan (Nonya) people living in Singapore.

The beginning of Nonya culture dates back to the 15th century in the port city of Malacca, then one of the world's great trading centers, situated on the Strait of Malacca.

The Nonya culture emerged when Chinese men who came to Malacca as traders settled there and married local Malay women. (Later there were also settlements in Penang.) These

Chinese-Malay intermarriages were the genesis of a new ethnic group and a fascinating subculture that locals call Peranakan or Straits Chinese. As the western term Eurasian is used to describe children of Caucasian and Asian parents, Peranakan or Straits Chinese identifies the offspring of Chinese-Malay marriages. Female offspring are referred to as *nonyas*, males as *babas*. As the number of Straits Chinese families grew, the two cultures mingled, until the customs, clothing, ceramics, architecture, and food of the Malay and Chinese were fused into a style and subculture called Nonya.

In the beginning Nonya cooking faced inherent obstacles. The Malays were primarily Muslim and foridden to eat pork, which was the staple meat of the Chinese. In addition, the Chinese men, who were primarily Hokkien from southern China, were used to foods cooked with dark soy sauce, fermented soy beans, garlic, leeks, and onions—foods that are country-style and robust compared to other southern Chinese cooking, but are relatively subtle next to heavily seasoned Malay cooking. After the first generation of intermarriage, Nonya girls tended to marry men from China or from other Straits Chinese communities, and eventually Chinese characteristics dominated Nonya cooking. Although some Muslim Malays do not eat pork, many Nonya and Chinese cooks apply Malay spicing techniques to the Chinese staple.

Nonya cooking is called Nonya because it is primarily food prepared in the home by women, the nonyas. The Malay wife taught her Chinese husband to enjoy curries and slow-simmered preparations. She introduced him to the aromatic tastes of fresh screwpine (*pandan*), fragrant lime (*limau perut*), fresh coriander leaves (*ketumbar*, common in Chinese cooking but mainly as a garnish), lemongrass (*serai*), and polygonum (*daun kesom*); the herbal overtones of galangal (*lengkuas*) and turmeric (*kunyit*); the intriguing sweet and citrus flavor of tamarind (*asam*); the pungent and savory taste of shrimp paste (*blachan*); and the richness and thickening characteristic of candlenuts (*buah keras*). She used coconut milk (*santen*), an indispensable ingredient throughout Southeast Asia, to mellow the rich, assertive, spicy edges of her food and bind together her mixtures.

Malay cooks borrow many Indian dried spices, but Nonya cooks use just a few, primarily coriander seeds (*ketumbar*) and cumin (*jintan puteh*); sometimes they add cardamom (*buah pelaga*) and fenugreek (*alma*) to special dishes. They appreciate the fiery brilliance of fresh and dried chiles, and use them freely. Mixing and blending these ingredients, the Nonya cook creates foods filled with intensity and fragrance, very different from the bland and subtle tastes of Chinese cooking.

The Chinese side of the marriage contributed fresh and dried noodles made from rice, wheat, and mungbean flour; fresh, dried, and fermented bean curd; and an array of Chinese vegetables. Nonya cooks also adopted Chinese fermented soybean pastes and sauces, dried black mushrooms and tree ear mushrooms, lily buds, bamboo shoots, and ginger as well as Chinese stir-frying, braising, and steaming techniques.

Nonya women were expected to master the complex art of cooking Nonya food as a prerequisite to marriage. Each had to perfect her technique for pounding dried spices and herbs on a *batu giling*, a flat granite grinding slab, which was the first step in making a *rempah*. Then she had to master *tumis*, the gentle frying of the ground spice blend. Every Nonya was expected to understand the properties of coconut milk, including how to grate, press, and cook it so that it did not curdle.

Today, Nonya food in Singapore reflects the styles of Malacca and Penang, as well as Indonesian touches from the Peranakan families that immigrated from Java and Sumatra. The Penang style is greatly influenced by its neighbor Thailand; the Malacca and Singapore styles reflect Indonesian influences.

The Straits Chinese are known for their extravagant style of entertaining, particularly the *Tok Panjang*, or "long table." On this literally "long table" are laid out a huge assortment of *gulais* (curries), *mee* (noodles), *sambals* (condiments), soups, and other traditional dishes. Guests are invited to take turns sitting at the table, serving themselves from a variety of dishes that are replenished as needed.

Nonya cuisine is also famous for its magnificent *kueh*—colorful, multi-layered cakes made from glutinous rice flour, coconut, and brown sugar. These brilliant, painstakingly produced creations have an unusually gummy or gelatin-like texture and shimmer with jelly bean color. They are cut into diamond-shaped, rainbow-colored pieces and served at tea time and for dessert. Unfortunately, master *kueh* bakers are a disappearing breed.

WHAT YOU NEED FOR COOKING SINGAPOREAN FOOD

The Asian kitchen is rather functional and unembellished. Few cooks have ovens and those who do use them to warm foods rather than to cook them. Most of the cooking is done on top of the stove. The basic cooking methods used in the Singapore kitchen are stir-frying, steaming, slow-braising in clay pots, deep-frying, grilling, and barbecuing. Grilling and barbecuing are particularly popular among Malay-Indonesian cooks.

You do not need to re-outfit your kitchen to cook Singaporean food, but a small investment in a few pieces of basic Asian cooking equipment and utensils will make the cooking easier and more fun.

WOK

A good old-fashioned wok (*kuali*) will enhance your cooking, but it is not essential; many Singaporean recipes are manageable in a skillet, saucepan, or small dutch oven. Still, if you try cooking in a wok, you will feel how naturally it fits with the food and the style of cooking.

Save your money and avoid electric, non-stick, fancy, aluminum, or stainless steel woks. If you decide to invest in a wok, go to a Chinese market and select a spun-steel wok, the kind that has faint thin rings around the surface. A 12- or 14-inch-wide wok is right for a home kitchen. If you have an electric stove, find a flat-bottom wok; it will sit securely on the hot coils, providing direct contact with the heat. A spun-steel wok must be seasoned before using.

To season a wok, first wash it with soap and water. If the factory-applied coating of machine oil does not come off, set the wok on the stove, fill it with hot water, and boil for a few minutes. Scour the wok for the first and last time with steel wool, dishwashing soap or cleanser (if needed), and hot water. Rinse well. Dry the wok over medium-high heat. As it is heating, it will change colors, creating irregular patterns of blue, purple, and orange. When the wok is hot enough that a few drops of water sprinkled in it sizzle and dance, pour in a few tablespoons of vegetable oil. Swirl the wok to coat the entire inner surface. Wad up a few paper towels and wipe off the excess oil. Reduce the heat to low and let the wok sit for 10 minutes. Turn off the heat and let the wok cool. The wok is now ready for use; with time and repeated use it will darken and take on a black patina.

To clean a wok after cooking, simply rinse well with hot water and scrape off foods with a soft-bristled brush. Do not use soap. If food gets burnt on, dry the surface, throw in a generous amount of coarse salt, and scour with wadded up paper towels, using the salt as an abrasive.

STEAMING BASKET

Many Singaporean dishes require steaming, a popular Chinese cooking method. A bamboo steaming basket with a cover should be part of a well-equipped kitchen. The steamer rests inside the wok, which is filled with hot water to 1 inch below the bottom of the basket. Choose a bamboo steamer 1 inch smaller in diameter than your wok; if you can afford a two-tier steamer, buy it.

SPICE GRINDER

A coffee grinder used only for grinding spices and either a blender or a mini-food processor for making spice pastes will surely save you time and effort.

EARTHENWARE POTS

Earthenware pots are traditionally used for braising and simmering, but the pots and pans in your kitchen will work equally well. Many clay pots are attractive enough to use for serving, and are not too costly.

OTHER EQUIPMENT

Although certainly not necessary, an Indian griddle, charcoal brazier or grill, and mortar and pestle will enhance your enjoyment of Singaporean cooking.

LEARN TO MAKE REMPAH

Rempah is the heart and soul of Malay-style and Nonya curries, sauces, and marinades. Many of the dishes in this book begin with a *rempah,* and you may suspect in reading the recipes that the finished dishes will have a sameness about them. They do not. While the *rempah* sets the theme that runs through much of Singaporean food, it is not a standard spice mix but an ever-changing combination of spices and aromatics that contributes to a rich and exciting variety of flavors and textures. Although the components change, the method remains consistent, so once you master the techniques for making a *rempah,* the exotic culinary world of Singapore will open to you.

Rempah is made by pounding a combination of "wet" and "dry" ingredients together to form a paste. The "dry" ingredients are spices such as coriander seeds, cumin, fenugreek, cloves, peppercorns, and cinnamon. The "wet" ingredients include fresh shallots, lemongrass, garlic, chiles, candlenuts, ginger, and *lengkuas.* The dry and wet ingredients are ground separately, then combined into a paste, which must be as smooth as possible.

It is of utmost importance in Singaporean cooking that the *rempah* is properly prepared. Making and frying a *rempah* is second nature to Asian cooks, and they tend to under-emphasize its importance when describing their art of cooking.

It is rather extraordinary to think that the traditional Nonyas, Malays, and Indonesians prepared their *rempahs* daily by pounding the ingredients by hand in a *batu leong* (a mortar and pestle) or a *batu giling* (a flat granite slab used with a rolling pin made of granite). With today's lifestyle, except for the sheer entertainment of it, the traditional method is unfeasible. Many old timers insist that a hand-ground *rempah* is far superior, and it probably is, but for the average American cook, an electric mini-food processor or blender and a spice grinder are the most efficient way to get the job done. Without these modern appliances, this style of cooking could easily have become extinct.

To facilitate the grinding of the wet ingredients, cut them into small pieces. If the appliance you use is up to it, you can throw all the wet ingredients in at once, add water, and grind to a smooth paste. With some mini-food processors, you may need to start with one ingredient, then add the others one by one; grind the hardest one first. When any of the following ingredients are used, I approach the grinding in this order, adding the dried spices after the wet ingredients are ground:

lengkuas (if dried, soak first and cut into small pieces)
lemongrass
fresh ginger
candlenuts
dried shrimp paste
garlic
shallots
leafy herbs and dried powdered spices

A few tablespoons of water help the paste come out smooth. What's needed more than precise guidelines is for you to experiment with your blender, processor, or electric grinder. Once you have established the formula that works best with your equipment, you will be able to grind your spice blend smoothly and efficiently.

To bring out the best flavor in your *rempah*, transfer the ground mixture to a mortar and pound and grind it for a minute with a pestle. Although this step is not required in the following recipes, the slight extra effort will always enhance your results. This last pounding will help you to approximate the traditional method of grinding which is better than modern appliances at extracting oils from the seed spices and forcing the mixture to marry.

TUMIS: FRYING THE *REMPAH*

Tumis means the gentle frying of the *rempah*. It is the second vital step in preparing a Singaporean "curry." Fresh oil is essential and so is the right amount of frying (*tumis*) time. It is best to fry in a preheated wok or saucepan over steady low to medium heat, continuously stirring to prevent the spice paste from sticking and burning.

Use the amount of oil called for in the recipe. It may seem like too much, but it is the minimum amount needed to fry the paste (see *A Word About Oil*, below). When you add the paste to the oil there should be a light bubbling sizzle. As you stir, the paste and oil should combine into a mixture like a thick tomato sauce. Continue frying the thick paste, stirring continuously, for 5 to 8 minutes. If the mixture begins to stick or become dry, add a tablespoon or two of water. When oil begins to seep out of the mixture (it will have a reddish hue if you used red chiles in the mixture), the *rempah* is cooked. If you stop frying too soon, the *rempah* will taste and smell raw.

Some *rempah* in this book start with the Straits Red Chile Paste on page 39, which is fried in the oil before the spice paste is added. When frying the Chile Paste, stir continuously and be careful not to burn it. Wait until the oil takes on a red color before adding the spice paste.

A WORD ABOUT OIL

Traditionally, lard was used in cooking *rempah*. Today most cooks use peanut, corn, soy, or other vegetable oils.

The amount of oil used to fry the *rempah* may seem excessive. Don't be alarmed or put off by it. The *rempah* needs the indicated amount of oil to keep it smooth and sauce-like during frying, and to bring out and mature each ingredient's flavor. Once the spice paste is fully cooked, the excess oil may be removed and discarded. A completely authentic *rempah* would actually call for a far greater amount of oil; in this book we have reduced the oil to the minimum amount needed to do the job properly.

Gulais, Malaysian-style curries, have red- or orange-tinged surface oil. The color cannot be achieved if the *rempah* is undercooked. So good color traditionally served as a gauge of whether a *gulai* was properly cooked. When there was no refrigeration in that part of the world, *gulais* were served out of large pots, warm or at room temperature; the surface oil, along with the spices, helped increase their "shelf life."

Fortunately, we are not faced with a lack of refrigeration. Once a dish is finished, all surface oils may be skimmed off and discarded.

A WORD ABOUT CHILES

Both fresh and dried chiles are called for in this book. At the Straits Cafe, the Red Chile Paste

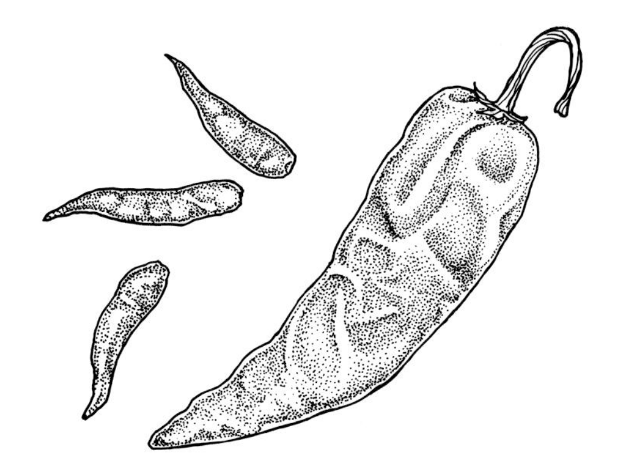

New Mexico (large) and Thai (small) dried chiles.

on page 39 is used as a cooking condiment and to color the cooking oil. To make it at home, use the dried red New Mexico chile which is sometimes referred to as "oil chile" for its robust red color and mild flavor. For fiery heat add dried Thai red chiles or dried cayenne chiles which may be found in Asian, Mexican, and better American supermarkets.

Before grinding dried chiles, always soak them in water to soften them. To reduce the heat of both fresh and dried chiles, cut the stems off and shake out and discard the seeds before soaking or using the chiles.

INGREDIENTS FOR THE SINGAPOREAN KITCHEN

Ingredients are listed alphabetically by the names by which they are known in Singapore. See the chart on page 44 for ingredient names in other languages. All of the following ingredients are part of the Singaporean pantry, whether the cook is Chinese, Malay, Nonya, or Indian.

ASAM (see Tamarind)

BAMBOO SHOOTS

Fresh bamboo shoots are difficult to find outside of Asia, so American cooks must resort to one of the canned varieties. Winter bamboo shoots are best; they are sweet, tender, and crisp. You can also use spring shoots and tips, which come in chunks, or the slices or julienned strips which are cut from large, coarse sprouts. Bamboo shoots may be used straight from the can after a thorough rinse with cold water. If they have a canned smell or taste, boil them in water for a minute, then rinse with cold water. Store unused shoots in the refrigerator in a container covered with fresh water and change the water every few days. Use within two weeks.

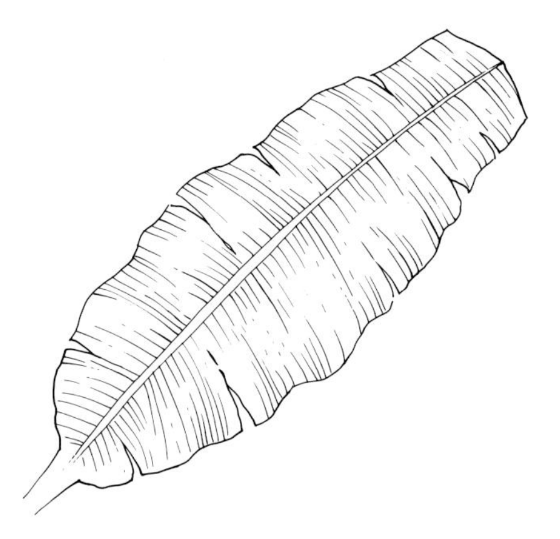

BANANA LEAVES

Asians use banana leaves to wrap foods for steaming or grilling much as Westerners use foil. Frozen leaves are available in Asian markets and fresh ones may be ordered from florists. (Some leaves have been sprayed, so be certain the florist knows you will be using them for cooking.) Rinse the leaves with cold water and clean them with a damp sponge before using. Cut away and discard the thick spine that runs the length of the leaf, then cut the leaf into the sizes you need.

Dip the pieces in boiling water for a few seconds to soften them; wipe them dry. After wrapping the ingredients and securing the ends of the package with sturdy toothpicks, you may reinforce the package with foil. If banana leaves are not available you can substitute foil, but the dish will lack the aromatic flavor imparted by the banana leaves.

BEAN CURD

The soybean has evolved into a variety of forms that range from fresh and dried bean curd cakes, squares, sheets, and sticks to fermented soybean cakes (*tempeh*), fermented bean curd (*fu yu*), and a host of bean sauces.

Fresh Bean Curd (Tofu)

Fresh bean curd has become so popular in America it can be found in the refrigerated or produce section of all major supermarkets. This fragile curd is made from soybeans that have been soaked, pureed, cooked, and solidified into curds with the help of *nigari* (magnesium chloride), a natural solidifier distilled from sea water. Bean curd is low in calories and cholesterol and high in protein. It is thought of as "the meat without bones" by its originators, the Chinese.

The two most common varieties are firm (hard) and soft. Firm bean curd can be stir-fried, deep-fried, or braised or can be stuffed then steamed, fried, or braised. Soft bean curd, which is silky and custard-like, can be eaten as is, chilled, with a dribble of oyster sauce or soy sauce and sesame or peanut oil. It can also be added to soups or can be slit open, stuffed with a lightly seasoned shrimp mousse, and steamed.

Store fresh bean curd in the refrigerator, covered with cold water. Change the water every few days. It should keep for a week.

Deep-Fried Bean Curd (Dou Fu Pok)

These are cubes of fresh firm bean curd that have been deep-fried until golden brown and crusty. During the frying the center hollows out, making them great for stuffing. Use them as is, throw them into a braised dish, or stir-fry them with noodles or vegetables. They also make a lovely edible garnish. To make your own, see page 166.

Dried Bean Curd Sheets or Sticks

When bean curd is made, a skin forms on top. It is removed, dried flat, and then folded into flat sheets or twisted into sticks. Before using, soak the sheets or sticks in warm water until soft and pliable. They are often added to stir-fried, braised, or soup dishes, sometimes as a substitute for meat. They can be stored in a dry pantry for several months; if they smell rancid, discard them.

Fermented Soybean Cake (Tempeh)

Tempeh is a nutritious, no-cholesterol, high-protein food made from fermented soybeans fashioned into a slab or sausage. A staple of the Indonesian kitchen, it has a crunchy texture and nut-like flavor. Store in the refrigerator for up to 3 weeks, or freeze for several months.

Bean (Soybean) Sauces

Throughout Asia soybeans are fermented and processed into sauces for use in cooking or as table condiments. Whole bean sauces, in which the beans are immersed in a thick brown liquid, are called either "bean sauce" or "brown bean sauce." The Malaysian variety, *tau cheo* (labelled "yellow bean sauce") is light tan in color; the Chinese variety ("brown bean sauce") is dark caramel brown. Both have a pungent, salty flavor and are used sparingly in cooking to add color and flavor and to help thicken sauces. "Ground bean sauce" is a mashed version of whole bean sauce. Whole and ground bean sauces are interchangeable.

Hoisin Sauce

Hoisin sauce is a prepared condiment made from soybeans, garlic, vinegar, and spices. *Hoisin* means fresh seafood. It is used at the table as a dipping sauce (see *Poh Pia,* page 58) or as a cooking seasoning. Hoisin sauce is available in jars or cans in Chinese markets. Store in a glass jar in the refrigerator. It keeps indefinitely.

BEAN SPROUTS, FRESH

Bean sprouts are sprouted from both mung beans and soybeans. Mung beans are more commonly used and are favored for their smaller sprouts. If time and your energy permit, remove the tail from each sprout before using.

BEE HOON (see Dried Chinese Rice Vermicelli)

BITTER MELON

Many consider this fruit an acquired taste. It is definitely bitter, but pleasantly so. Asian cooks treat it like a vegetable, steaming, stuffing, stir-frying, or deep-frying it, or making it into soup. When unripe, the fat, squat fruit is a deep green color with a waxy, alligator-like skin. Its body comes to a point at one end and has a stem like a long skinny tail at the other. To prepare a bitter melon for cooking, cut it in half lengthwise and scrape out and discard the pulp. For stuffing, cut it crosswise into sections and scrape out the pulp. Unfortunately, if fresh bitter melon is not available, there is no substitute.

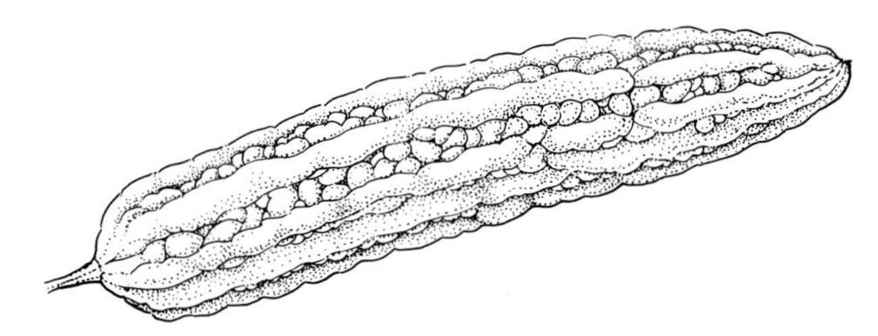

BLACHAN (see Shrimp Paste, Dried)

BLACK PEPPERCORNS

The quest for black pepper and other exotic spices indigenous to Indonesia has been a theme in world history for a very long time. Even in antiquity Arab and Indonesian traders made hazardous voyages across the Indian Ocean and over difficult terrain to trade in such Southeast Asian spices as pepper, cinnamon, ginger, cloves, nutmeg, and cassia as well as aromatic resins and woods to be used for incense and medicines. Black pepper, the world's most commonly used spice, was the main source of peppery heat in Asian cooking until the Portuguese introduced the chile pepper around the middle of the 16th century. Despite their love of fresh chiles, Asian cooks still use a lot of black pepper.

CANDLENUTS

Originally used in candle making, candlenuts (*buah keras*) are valued for their thickening ability and for their oil in Malaysian and Indonesian cooking. They are an essential ingredient in *rempah*; raw candlenuts are toxic, so *rempah* must always be cooked. Candlenuts are now widely available in Southeast Asian markets. It is best to keep them frozen. Soak them in warm water a few minutes before grinding them into a spice blend. If you can't find candlenuts, substitute blanched almonds or macadamia nuts.

CARDAMOM

A member of the ginger family, cardamom is indigenous to India and Sri Lanka. The cardamom pod—white when bleached, pale green when dried in the oven, or brown when dried in the sun—contains clusters of seeds, about six per cluster. The seeds have a lemony-eucalyptus flavor. Many Malay and Nonya *rempahs* contain cardamom seeds. Store the pods in a jar in a cool, dry place with minimal light. They should keep for about a year.

CHILES, FRESH AND DRIED

The recipes in this book use six types of chiles, three fresh and three dried. All are readily available in American markets. They are not exactly the same as the Asian varieties used in Singapore, but those are hard to find here, even in large Asian markets. The fresh varieties used at the Straits Cafe and in this book are Fresno (red, yellow, and green) and jalapeño (red and green) for stuffing and serrano (red and green) for heat. The three dried chiles are New Mexico red chile for color and whole dried cayenne or *chile de árbol* for heat. (See Red Chile Paste, page 39.)

CHINESE CELERY

Singaporean cooks prefer the leaves and stems of Chinese celery to their Western counterparts because of their stronger celery flavor. They use them in soups and stews. The stems are long and thin; the leaves are flat, jagged, and very similar to the European variety. Use and store as you would domestic celery.

CHINESE CHIVES (see Onions)

CHINESE SAUSAGE

Chinese sausages are used frequently in Singaporean cooking, particularly in noodle dishes. They are made of ground pork, cured with a strong Chinese wine and seasoned with sugar and light spices. They are hard and dark red in color, like dry Italian salami, and are sweet tasting rather than savory. They come with embedded bits of fat, without the fat, or with tiny morsels of cured duck liver. To cook, simply steam them for 15 minutes, then slice them diagonally and serve as an appetizer, toss with stir-fried noodles, or dice and use in a filling for *Poh Pia* spring rolls (page 58). Look for them in Asian markets. Store in the refrigerator for a few weeks or freeze for several months. There are no substitutes.

CINNAMON

Cinnamon is an essential spice in many curry dishes and some aromatic soups. Sometimes cassia is sold as cinnamon; they are not the same. Cinnamon is the bark or "sweet wood" from the evergreen cinnamon tree of Sri Lanka. It is pale tan and has a delicate flavor. Cassia is indigenous to Indonesia and China; it is dark reddish brown and has a strong warm and sweet flavor. Stick cinnamon retains its pungency indefinitely. Ground cinnamon is not used in recipes in this book.

CLOVES

Cloves are the dried flower buds of a tree of the myrtle family. They came originally from the Molucca islands of Indonesia. Today about 80 percent of our cloves come from Zanzibar; the rest come from Madagascar and Brazil. Cloves are frequently used in Indian, Indonesian, Malaysian, and Thai cooking. Store them in an airtight container away from light; they will keep indefinitely.

COCONUT MILK (and COCONUT CREAM)

Coconut milk is not the liquid in the middle of the nut; that is coconut juice. Coconut milk is an extraction made by mixing grated coconut flesh with hot water and squeezing the liquid out of the coconut meat. Coconut milk is used throughout Southeast Asia and Indonesia to thicken sauces, add flavor, and tame hot, spicy ingredients. Fresh homemade coconut milk is best; however, not all American cooks have fresh grated coconut meat available in markets within easy walking distance as cooks in Asia do. Good quality canned coconut milk, such as Chaokoh brand from Thailand, produces very good results. There is no substitute for coconut milk.

Coconut milk can be refrigerated in a plastic container for a few days or frozen for several weeks after opening.

For coconut cream, do not shake the can before opening. Pour the contents of the can into a tall glass container. Let it sit until the liquid separates, then skim off the "cream" from the top. The liquid that has settled to the bottom may be used as thin coconut milk.

For thick coconut milk, shake the can before opening and use as is.

For medium coconut milk, dilute thick coconut milk with half as much water.

For thin coconut milk, dilute thick coconut milk with an equal amount of water.

CORIANDER, FRESH (CILANTRO)

Asian cooks use all the parts of the coriander plant. They toast and grind the seeds for spice blends, use the leaves as an herb, and use the roots to flavor Thai curry pastes and Malaysian curries. You can use stems in place of roots, but there is no substitute for the fresh leaves. Coriander plants are easily grown from seed.

CORIANDER SEEDS

These khaki-colored round seeds are actually the fruit of the coriander plant. They have a delightful perfumy aroma and are used frequently in spice blends in Indonesian, Malaysian, Indian, and Thai cooking. To obtain the best results, dry-toast the seeds in a skillet or in the oven until aromatic, then grind them. Store like other dry spices. The whole seeds will keep for almost two years; ground, they will keep for a few months.

CUMIN SEEDS

Part of the parsley family, cumin seeds have a robust, hearty aroma and flavor. They are often a main component in curry spice blends. It is important to toast cumin seeds in a dry pan before grinding them. Store in an airtight container away from light in a cool, dry place.

CURRY (KARI) LEAVES

A Tamil word, *kari* means seasoned sauce. The fresh leaves are shiny, bright green and look like miniature lemon leaves with serrated edges. They can be found in Indian grocery stores. A "sprig of leaves" means about 10 to 12 leaves. The leaves may be refrigerated for up to two weeks or frozen for several months. Don't bother with store-bought dried leaves; unless they are aromatic when cracked they will lack flavor. It is better to buy fresh leaves and dry what you don't use.

CURRY POWDER

Curry powder is a commercially prepared blend of spices and seasonings. The mix can contain a few ingredients or as many as 20 or more spices and herbs. You can expect a blend to contain a balanced combination of a few, several, or perhaps all of the following spices: cumin, coriander, fenugreek, cloves, turmeric, black peppercorns, cardamom, cinnamon, ginger, mace, and cayenne. To make the recipes in this book, select a curry powder from India sold in a specialty food store; a yellow (turmeric) curry powder is preferable. Store in an airtight container in a cool, dry spot away from light.

DAUN KESOM

Daun kesom is a pungent herb casually referred to as laksa leaves. Its long, thin, dark green blades come to a point and have a strong, eucalyptus-like, biting fragrance and taste. It can be found fresh in better Asian markets under its Vietnamese name *rau ram* or as Vietnamese mint. There is no adequate substitute, but do try the *Laksa Lemak* on page 71 even if you can't find it; use a bit of mint in its place.

DAUN LIMAU PERUT (KAFFIR LIME LEAVES)

The popularity of Thai cooking in the United States has brought kaffir lime to the attention of American cooks. The fruit, indigenous to Southeast Asia, has a wart-like dark green rind which imparts a perfumy aroma, flavor, and oil to Thai food. The leaves, also known as fragrant lime leaf by Singaporean, Malay-Indonesian, and Nonya cooks, are valued for the fragrance and aromatic flavor they contribute in cooking. The juice is used in non-food products, such as shampoo.

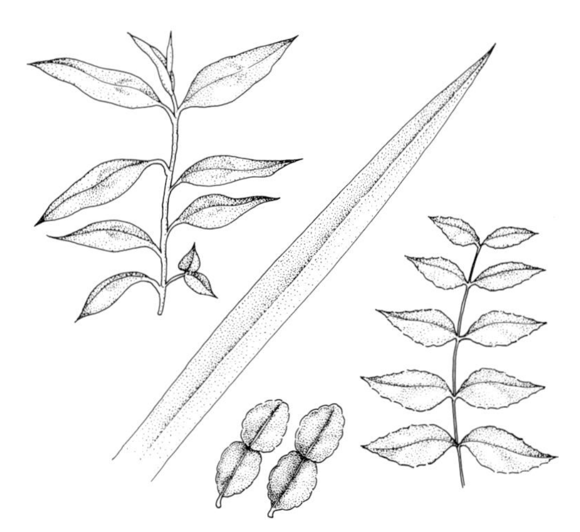

Left to right: daun kesom, daun pandan, daun limau perut, curry leaves.

The leaves are mostly available dried, but you may find them fresh or frozen in better Southeast Asian food stores. Soak the dried leaves about 5 minutes before tossing them into soups, stews, and curries, as you would bay leaves. Fresh leaves from other citrus trees are another alternative.

DAUN PANDAN

Pandan leaves, also known as screwpine leaves, are common in Southeast Asian cooking. They are used primarily in desserts. They impart a strong vanilla-like flavor and a deep emerald-green color to food. They can be found in Asian markets, usually in the frozen food section. Simply wipe them clean before using and scrape the blades with a fork to help release their flavor, fragrance, and color.

DRIED BLACK MUSHROOMS

Chinese "dried black forest mushrooms" have come to be known by their Japanese name, *shiitake* mushrooms. (The Chinese prefer them dried; the Japanese cook them dried and fresh.) A common Asian ingredient, they come in several varieties ranging from light tan to black in color. The best grade are whole, perfectly shaped light tan caps with a speckled flower-like pattern. The dried mushrooms come in cellophane bags and must be soaked in water, rinsed, drained, and squeezed dry before using. Cut off and discard the stems. The soaking water may be used in stocks or sauces. Store dried mushrooms in an airtight container at room temperature.

DRIED SHRIMP

Drying intensifies the flavor of shrimp, making them a wonderful source of seafood flavor. Dried shrimp can be found in the Asian and Mexican food sections of large supermarkets. They come in various sizes; the smallest, about ¼ inch long, are called "rice-size shrimp." Look for pinkish shrimp about 1 inch long. Avoid any that are grey; they are old. Dried shrimp can often be used as is, but for some dishes they must be soaked in warm water for 30 minutes then drained. Dried shrimp will keep indefinitely in a well-sealed container at room temperature.

FENNEL SEEDS

Fennel seeds are similar to cumin seeds. They are the same shape, but are larger, lighter in color, and have a strong anise flavor. Store them in an airtight container in a cool, dry spot away from light.

FISH SAUCE (see Thai Fish Sauce)

FIVE-SPICE POWDER

Despite its name, this blend may combine six or seven spices. A good version should have star anise, cinnamon, cloves, fennel or anise seeds, and ginger or, depending on the blender, Sichuan peppercorns. The sweet pungent flavors of cinnamon and anise dominate. Store in an airtight container in a cool, dry spot away from light.

GALANGAL (see *Lengkuas*)

GARAM MASALA

The term *masala* means spice blend. Garam masala is the aromatic "warm" blend of dry-roasted spices and herbs used in Indian cooking. The mix may include some or all of the following in various quantities: cardamom, coriander seeds, cumin seeds, cloves, black peppercorns, dried chiles, and cinnamon. Garam masala is thought to stimulate or "warm" internal body heat. It is generally added to a dish just before serving. There are many commercially prepared brands from India that are very good. It will last up to six months in an airtight container.

GARLIC

The only form of garlic called for in this book is fresh peeled cloves. Trim the root tip of each clove before slicing, chopping, or pounding it into a *rempah.*

GINGER

Ginger in this book means fresh ginger. When a slice is called for in a recipe, cut a slice about the size of a quarter (1 inch diameter, 1/16 inch thick). To help release its flavor, juice, and aroma, bruise or crush the slice by slapping it with the side of a cleaver. Peel the ginger by scraping it with a vegetable peeler or with the square edge of a bamboo chopstick before mincing, shredding, or grating it. For ginger juice, press ginger slices through a garlic press and catch the juice in a small bowl. Store ginger in a brown paper bag in the vegetable bin in the refrigerator. It will keep for several weeks.

HOISIN SAUCE (see page 28)

IKAN BILIS

Ikan Bilis is a very small species of anchovy, often incorrectly referred to as whitebait, which is dried and deep-fried until crisp. Mixed with roasted peanuts and seasoned with salt and sugar, it is a typical Malaysian appetizer served before a meal with drinks. It also accompanies *Nasi Lemak* (see page 83) as a side dish to eat with rice. It may be found in Southeast Asian markets.

KECAP MANIS (see Soy Sauce)

KEMIRI (see Candlenuts)

KRUPUK

Krupuk is a generic term for a broad range of crispy chips from Indonesia. The name specifically refers to shrimp chips, the most common type of krupuk. A batter is made from tapioca flour, eggs, and salt, blended with shrimp, fish, rice, or a nut-like fruit called *malinjo,* which is the most interesting taste of all. The batter is steamed then sliced and allowed to dry in the sun until the slices are totally dehydrated and look like tough wafers. Before serving, the dried wafers are tossed into hot oil. Within seconds they puff up and expand to at least triple their size. They make a great appetizer or may be served as a bread or even as a serving plate (see recipe, page 168).

LASKA LEAVES (see *Daun Kesom*)

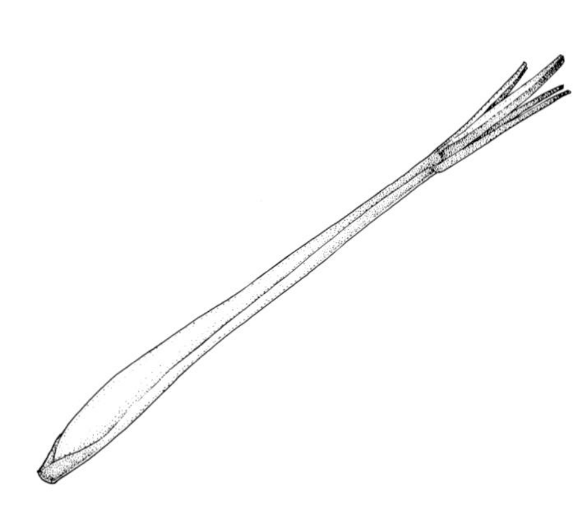

Lemongrass

LEMONGRASS

Lemongrass is an essential component of Southeast Asian cooking. It is a thin, solid, scallion-like plant with a delightful lemony flavor and scent. Lemongrass is now available almost all year round in Asian and American markets. To use it, remove the tough, fibrous outer leaves until you reach the purple ring at its tender, bulb-like heart. Use about the last 4 inches above the trimmed root end. Slap the stalk with the side of a cleaver to help release its flavor. Dried stems of lemongrass are also available, but they are pretty flavorless. If you can't get fresh lemongrass, substitute a long strip of fresh lemon peel for each stalk of lemongrass called for.

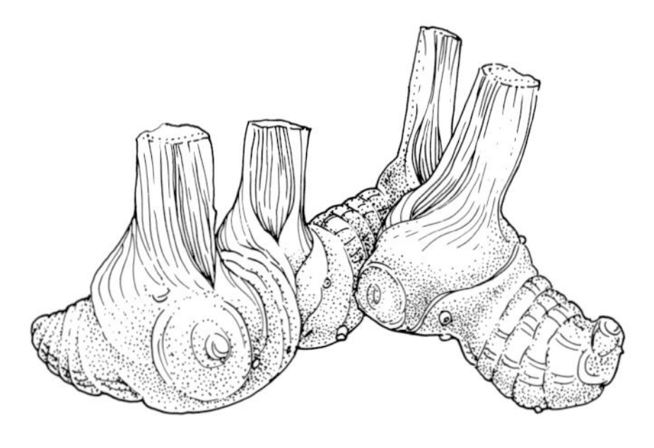

Lengkuas

LENGKUAS

Lengkuas, made popular through Thai cooking, is better known in the United States by its Thai name, *kha,* or its English name, galangal. It is essential to Nonya, Malay, and Indonesian cooking; there is no suitable substitute.

This rhizome, a member of the ginger family, imparts a faint medicinal flavor and has a slight mustard fragrance. It can be found both fresh and dried in better Asian markets. If you use dried slices, always soak them in warm water at least 30 minutes, until soft and pliable, before using them. It is virtually impossible to grind or chop dried lengkuas in a food processor before it is reconstituted in water. If you use fresh lengkuas in a recipe that calls for dried, use two or three times as much as called for. To measure fresh lengkuas, scrape off the thin skin with a vegetable peeler then cut 1-inch rounds, about 1/16 inch thick (the size of a U.S. quarter). Store fresh lengkuas in a brown paper bag in the vegetable bin in the refrigerator; it will keep for a few weeks. Frozen it will keep for several months.

LESSER GINGER POWDER

Lesser ginger, known as *kentjur* in Indonesia and *krachai* in Thailand, is a small finger-size rhizome used in curries and salads throughout Southeast Asia. It is a relative of common ginger and galangal (*lengkuas*), but its taste is milder and somewhat medicinal; its primary use in Asia is medicinal. Dried and powdered *kentjur* is available in Asian markets. If you can't find it, omit it from the recipe; there is no substitute.

LILY BUDS, DRIED

Lily buds are the unopened flower buds of the orange day lily plant. They are sold in cellophane bags. Look for pale gold buds that are soft and pliable. They must be soaked in warm water before using. Pick off and discard the hard ends. Store lily buds in a well-sealed plastic bag in the refrigerator or in an airtight jar in the cupboard. They will keep for several months.

LIMES

Limes inject a zesty, tart flavor into soups, salads, noodles, and chile sambals. Cooks in Asia use a local round, golf-ball-size lime called by its Malay name, *limau kesturi*. It is very much like the *kalamansi* lime of the Philippines. Do not confuse this lime with "fragrant lime," also known as kaffir lime (see *daun limau perut*), which is desired for its rind and leaves but not necessarily its juice. Our familiar fresh lime may be substituted for *limau kesturi* in recipes, although it is not quite the same.

NOODLES

Although it is debatable whether Marco Polo discovered noodles in China and brought them back to Italy, we do know that noodles were brought from southern China to the rest of Asia. The noodles used in Singaporean cooking are Chinese style, made from wheat, wheat and egg, rice, or mung beans. All come in both fresh and dried forms except mung bean, which comes only dried.

To cook 1 pound of fresh wheat flour noodles, bring 4 quarts of salted water to a boil in a wok or large stockpot over high heat. Gently pull the ball of noodles apart to separate the strands, then add them to the water. Stir with long chopsticks to separate the strands. When the water reaches a second boil, add 1 cup of cold water to the pot. Continue cooking 1 minute longer, then pour the noodles into a colander. Rinse thoroughly with cold water. Drain, shaking off all excess water.

Do not thaw frozen noodles. Simply take them out of the bag in a solid piece and add them to boiling salted water. Stir continuously with chopsticks until the strands are separated, and continue as for fresh noodles.

Wheat Flour Based Noodles

Chinese Wheat Flour Noodles are made with wheat flour and supposedly no egg. Wheat flour noodles are confusing in that some manufacturers do add egg, but not enough to call them true Chinese egg noodles. Available fresh and dried in American supermarkets, they are labelled "chow mein" or simply "Chinese noodles." They look like a bundle of smooth, beige spaghetti-like strands.

These all-purpose noodles may be used for stir-frying, deep-frying, and soups.

Chinese Egg Noodles are also found in American supermarkets. They are made from wheat flour, eggs, and water. They are egg-yellow and come in medium (spaghetti-size) and thin (spaghettini-size) widths. Both sizes have slightly twisted strands that work well for stir-frying, deep-frying, soups, and cold noodle salads.

The thin egg noodles contain more egg than medium-width noodles and have a heartier texture, making them better for soups and chilled noodle dishes. In a pinch, thin noodles can also be stir-fried or shallow-fried, but sauces cling to and are absorbed better by the medium-width noodles. Store fresh egg noodles in the refrigerator for up to a week or freeze them up to three months.

Fresh Yellow "Hokkien" Noodles These fresh, thick-spaghetti-size Chinese egg noodles are popular with Hokkien cooks and are also used by Indian and Malay cooks. They have a very rich yellow color. True Hokkien *mee* (noodles) are not available in America, but basic Chinese egg noodles (medium width) work well in their place.

Rice Flour Noodles

Rice flour noodles are immensely popular among Asians for their silky-smooth texture and mild flavor. They are made from a fine rice flour and water batter which is spread in a thin, even layer on a cloth stretched across a steam tray, or on shallow pizza pan-like trays, a modern adaptation. Fresh rice noodles are available in Chinese markets in whole, flat rolled-up sheets to wrap around a shrimp or meat filling like cannelloni or pre-cut into flat fettuccine-like ribbons. Keep them refrigerated and use within five days. They do not freeze well.

Flat Ribbon Noodles (Kway Teow) are fresh, flat, fettuccine-size ribbon noodles (about 3/8 inch wide) used for stir-frying or in soups.

"Laksa" Rice Noodles are fresh rice noodles that resemble opaque white spaghetti. They are popular in coconut milk curry sauces and soups. Keep them refrigerated. Before using, blanch them in boiling water for a minute and drain. Fresh laksa noodles should be used within a few days. You may substitute dried rice vermicelli; it will be quite different in taste and texture, but still good.

Dried Chinese Rice Vermicelli (Bee Hoon) Also called rice stick noodles, these dried noodles are made from rice flour. They are wiry, thin, and brittle looking. After being softened in water, they can be stir-fried or added to curry dishes and soups. They can also be deep-fried in oil without pre-soaking; puffy and crispy, the fried noodles add texture to salads or can be used as a bed for stir-fried meats and vegetables. Store dried noodles in a dry cupboard.

Mung Bean Thread Noodles

These noodles look like wiry, thin, brittle white threads wound up into a bundle. Actually, the dried noodles are so tough they cannot be cut before being rehydrated. They are made from mung bean puree that is strained and dried into sheets or noodles. Mung bean noodles are often simmered with meats and vegetables or served cold in salads. They can also be boiled and immersed in soup or can be deep-fried in their dried form to make puffy, crisp noodles.

Bean thread noodles have several names; they may be labelled transparent, cellophane, glass, mirror, or peastarch noodles, or even (in Hawaii) "long rice." Do not confuse them with dried rice noodles, which look quite similar. It is best to check the ingredient list on the package to be sure you are buying the correct noodle. There will be many times when you need only a few ounces, so it is convenient to buy them in an 8-pack bag of individually wrapped 1½-ounce bundles. Store the dry noodles in an airtight plastic bag in a dry cupboard.

To prepare bean thread noodles, place the required amount of noodles in a bowl. Cover them with warm water and let them soak for about 20 minutes or until they are soft and pliable. Drain. The noodles are ready to stir-fry, simmer, or add to soups. When cooked they become transparent and gelatinous.

OILS, COOKING

Ghee

Ghee is one of the preferred traditional cooking oils of Indian cooks. It is made from clarified unsalted butter (butter with the milk solids removed). The clarified butter is simmered slowly until all the moisture evaporates and the residual sugar slightly caramelizes, creating a nutty, aromatic flavored oil with a higher burning temperature than butter (170°F). It is excellent for sauteing. Ghee may be found in Indian markets, or you can make your own as described above; it will keep for several months in the refrigerator, or longer in the freezer.

Peanut Oil

Asian cooks prefer peanut oil because of its high smoking point and neutral flavor. Corn oil also works exceptionally well for Asian cooking.

Sesame Oil, Asian

Asian sesame oil differs from Western sesame oil in that the oil is pressed from toasted sesame seeds. Toasting brings out a nutty flavor and aroma. It is used sparingly as a seasoning oil and is not meant for cooking.

ONIONS

Chinese Chives

Chinese chives have a delicate garlic-like flavor, stronger than the flavor of Western chives. They are a foot or more long and have slender, flat, dark green blades. Cut them into shorter lengths before using them in spring rolls and dumpling fillings or stir-frying them with meats, eggs, or noodles. Because they are very delicate, they should always be added during the last seconds of cooking.

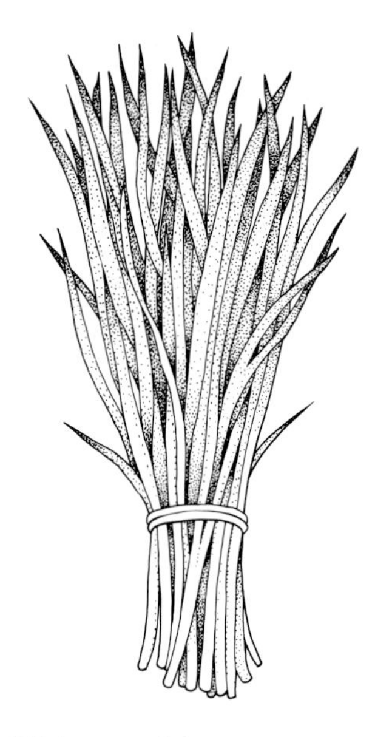
Chinese chives

Green Onions
Green onions, a staple in Chinese cooking, are used throughout Asia. In the eastern U.S. they are known as scallions or spring onions. Asian cooks use the green tops as well as the white bulbs.

Shallots
Shallots are the onions commonly used in Malay-Indonesian, Indian, and Nonya cooking in Singapore. They are also the preferred onion in Thailand, Laos, and Vietnam. They are an essential ingredient in *rempah.* The recipes in this book were developed with American-size shallots (the size of a small walnut in the shell), which are about twice the size of the shallots used in Asia. You may substitute yellow (Spanish) onions, one medium onion for each four shallots.

OYSTER SAUCE
A bottled sauce, oyster sauce has a concentrated, savory taste that is not at all fishy. It is used as seasoning or as a dipping sauce. Think of oyster sauce as a high-quality bouillon cube; adding a few teaspoons to a dish automatically converts a water-based sauce into a savory sauce. However, because it is an extract it should be used with discretion. Look for brands that are not pasty or lumpy-thick, but smooth, rich, and evenly colored. Refrigerated, it will keep indefinitely.

PANDAN LEAF (see *Daun Pandan*)

PICKLED SHALLOTS
Pickled shallots are available in jars or cans. They are not actually shallots, but a small onion variety from China. They look like fat white scallion bulbs. Pickled sweet-and-sour style, they are refreshing accompaniments.

PLUM SAUCE
Plum sauce is a chutney-like condiment made from plums, apricots, chiles, vinegar, and sugar. It is sometimes called duck sauce, because it is served with roast duck. It is often confused with hoisin sauce, which is served with Peking duck and mu shu pork. Plum sauce is available in jars or cans in Chinese markets. Store it in a glass jar in the refrigerator. It keeps indefinitely.

POH PIA SKINS (see Spring Roll Wrappers)

POPPADUMS
Also known as Indian flat bread, poppadums (also spelled pappadams) are made from various dried split-pea or *dal* flours mixed with pepper, chiles, and garlic or other seasonings. They are

thin and brittle and look like dried flat tortillas. When you submerge the dried disks in hot oil, they will puff up within seconds into crispy crackers twice their original size. Serve them as bread in an Indian meal.

RED CHILE PASTE

In the kitchen of the Straits Cafe there is a large stainless steel container filled to the brim with a beautiful mahogany-red chile paste. Chris makes a fresh batch of chile paste to replenish the container daily. It is strategically stationed next to the wok stove. The cooks instinctively dip a ladle into the chile paste, flip it into a wok, and cook it gently to develop its flavor and heighten its color. It is indispensable to the Straits Cafe and to all Singaporean kitchens, just as wine is to French kitchens.

To make a small batch of Red Chile Paste (about ½ to ⅔ cup) cut 5 dried red New Mexico or California chiles and 5 small dried Thai red or cayenne chiles into pieces with kitchen shears. Discard the stems and seeds. Put the chiles into a saucepan, cover them with water, and bring the pot to a boil. Cook at a low boil until soft, about 5 minutes. Drain and cool. Puree the chiles in a blender or food processor. Store Red Chile Paste in a jar, top with a thin layer of vegetable oil, and refrigerate for a few days.

In a pinch, *Sambal Oelek*, a commercially prepared red chile paste, may be substituted. It is much hotter, so use half as much.

RICE

In Asia rice is not only food, it is a symbol of life. Having an abundance of rice at a meal is a statement of well-being. Asians prefer white rice milled of its bran layer. They use three varieties: short-grain, long-grain, and glutinous rice.

Glutinous (Sweet) Rice

Glutinous rice does not taste particularly sweet. It is called sweet rice because it is used for sweet dessert dishes. It is also referred to as sticky rice because when cooked it takes on a sticky, glutinous consistency. In Thailand it is preferred over long-grain rice for everyday eating at main meals. The Thais shape the cooked rice into a ball with their fingers and eat it straight out of hand. The Chinese use sweet rice to stuff poultry or wrap it in bamboo or lotus leaves to form dumplings. Black glutinous rice, which still contains its bran layer, has a nutty flavor and is used primarily for desserts in Southeast Asia. It is not the same as brown rice.

Long-Grain Rice

Long-grain rice is the preferred rice throughout Asia, except in Japan, the Philippines, and parts of Thailand. Properly cooked long-grain rice should lightly adhere together, but the lumps of rice should fall apart with a slight nudge from a pair of chopsticks. In Singapore long-grain rice is sometimes cooked with coconut milk (see *Nasi Lemak*, page 83) or colored with turmeric to make the Malay dish *Nasi Kunyit* (page 84).

Short-Grain Rice

Short-grain rice tends to stick together more than long-grain but is not nearly as sticky as sweet rice. It generally takes less cooking water than long-grain. Short-grain rice is preferred by the Japanese for everyday eating and for sushi.

RICE FLOUR

Rice flour is made from long-grain rice. Sold as "rice powder" in Asian markets, it is used as a binder and thickener. Store it as you would other flours. Do not confuse it with glutinous rice flour, which is used for desserts.

SHIITAKE MUSHROOMS (see Dried Black Mushrooms)

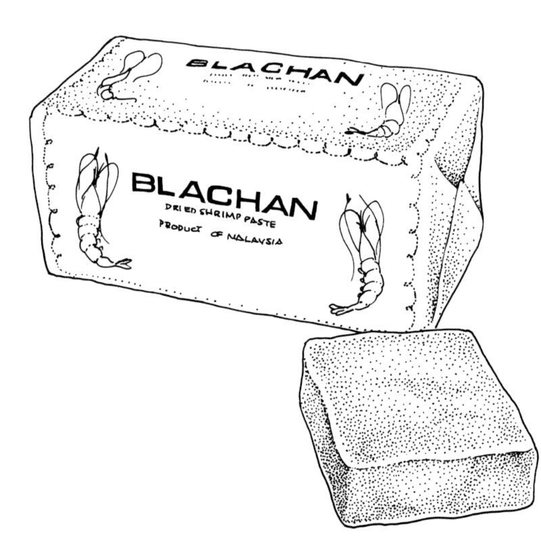

SHRIMP PASTE, DRIED (BLACHAN)

Blachan, dried fermented shrimp paste, is one of the most mysterious and perhaps formidable ingredients in Southeast Asian cooking. It is made from pounded shrimp saturated with salt and allowed to ferment.

It comes in various forms. The mushy pink wet paste packed in jars tends to be Chinese-style shrimp paste; the dried slabs that range from dark purple to black-brown and come wrapped in tissue-thin paper or plastic are popular in Southeast Asia. The wet paste, which should be stored in the refrigerator, can be used raw. The dried varieties must be cooked, either by frying in an ungreased pan or by molding a piece on the tip of a metal skewer and grilling it directly over the fire. If the shrimp paste is to be fried with other spices, preliminary cooking is not necessary. If you want to pan-fry a large amount of shrimp paste (a few ounces) it is a good idea to wrap the pieces in foil first to contain the very pungent odor, then dry-fry it in the foil. Store the unused portion in a glass jar with a tight-fitting lid in a cool, dry place. Shrimp paste will keep indefinitely. (*See also* Thick Shrimp Paste)

SOY SAUCE

Soy sauce is the basic seasoning of Chinese cooking. Its use extends throughout Asia. The varieties of soy sauce seem to be limitless and are often confusing. It is important to select naturally fermented soy sauce, otherwise you may wind up with salted colored water which is totally flavorless. The main soy sauce varieties used in this book are light or thin soy sauce, dark or black soy sauce, sweet soy sauce (from Thailand), and Indonesian-style soy sauce called *kecap manis*.

Dark Soy Sauce

Dark soy sauce is a bit thicker and much darker than light soy sauce and has a richer, more complex, savory and sweet flavor.

Light Soy Sauce

Light soy sauce has a delicate flavor but tends to be saltier than dark soy sauce. It is often used as a table soy sauce.

Sweet Soy Sauce

Thai sweet soy sauce tastes like dark soy sauce but, as its name suggests, it has a sweeter edge.

Kecap Manis (pronounced Ketchup Manis)

This thick, syrupy-sweet soy sauce from Indonesia makes a delicious dipping sauce or table condiment. It is soy sauce blended with molasses or palm sugar and sometimes garlic, spices, and herbs. Bottles of *kecap manis* (also spelled *ketjap manis*) can be found in Southeast Asian grocery stores. It keeps well in an airtight container.

SPRING ROLL WRAPPERS

Spring roll wrappers can be found in the frozen food sections of Asian markets. We recommend Menlo brand for *Poh Pia* (Nonya-style fresh spring rolls, page 58) and Samosas (page 52). If Menlo is not available, look for 8-inch square or round wrappers that do not contain egg; the eggless skins are tastier for "fresh" (not fried) spring rolls.

SRIRACHA CHILE SAUCE

A variety of commercially prepared chile dipping sauces used in Asia are available in markets here. One of the most popular is the fiery sriracha sauce from Thailand. It is used primarily as a table sauce.

STAR ANISE

Star anise, a native of China, is an eight-pointed star-shaped pod from a tree in the magnolia family. It is favored for its strong anise flavor. Store in an airtight container in a cool, dry spot away from light. It should last indefinitely.

SWEET PICKLED GINGER

Young ginger has a soft texture and mild flavor. When sweet pickled, it takes on a pale pink color. It is particularly good with raw fish dishes (see *Yu Sang,* page 55) and salads. Look for it in jars in Asian markets. It will keep indefinitely in the refrigerator.

TAMARIND

Fresh tamarind pods are 4 to 6 inches long. They are kiwi brown and look like pregnant green beans. The pulp has a fruity sweet and sour flavor like prunes. The entire pod is used in some dishes, but most often the pod is cracked and the pulp is removed, soaked in hot water, and pressed through a strainer to make tamarind water. The seeds and pulp are then discarded. Tamarind pulp is also available in 8-ounce packages. It contains some seeds and fibers, and works well in place of fresh pods.

To make tamarind water, cut 2 ounces of tamarind pulp into ½-inch pieces. Cover the pulp with 3 cups of boiling water and soak for 15 minutes. Mash the pulp and separate the fibers and seeds with the back of a fork. When the pulp is fully softened, pour it into a strainer over a bowl; use the back of a spoon to force the pulp through and press out the liquid. Scrape the pulp clinging to the underside of the strainer into the bowl. Discard the seeds and fibers. Makes about 2½ cups. Store, covered, in the refrigerator for up to 10 days. Or freeze in ice cube trays, unmold into a freezer bag, and store frozen for up to two months.

You can also get jars of tamarind concentrate, which you dilute with hot water. Its flavor is barely satisfactory, so use it only in a pinch.

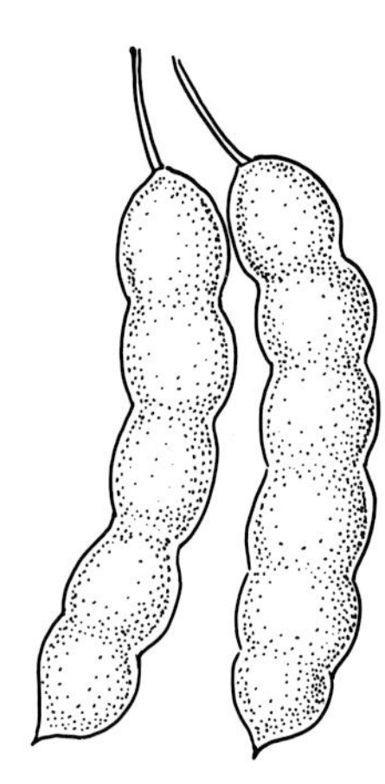

Tamarind pod

TEMPEH (see Fermented Soybean Cake, page 27)

THAI FISH SAUCE (NAM PLA)

This Southeast Asian equivalent of soy sauce is translucent, dark brown, and very thin. It has a salty flavor and a pungent smell that dissipates during cooking. Stored in an airtight container in the cupboard it will keep indefinitely.

THICK SHRIMP PASTE

Do not confuse this with dried shrimp paste. Thick shrimp paste is a sweet, treacle-like paste used as a condiment or for making the sauce for *rujak,* a Malay-Indonesian vegetable salad.

TOFU (see Fresh Bean Curd, page 27)

TURMERIC

Yellow is traditionally a sacred color in Southeast Asia and India. Turmeric contributes the bright orange-yellow color and a musty flavor to Indian, Malaysian-Indonesian, and Thai curries. It is a rhizome, a cousin to the ginger family, but it does not have the pungency of ginger. It is generally sold in its powdered form; however, fresh turmeric is now available in better Asian markets. To use fresh turmeric, peel it and crush it in a mortar with other spices. Store fresh turmeric in a dry paper bag in the refrigerator. Store powdered turmeric in an airtight container in a cool, dry spot away from light.

WATER CHESTNUT FLOUR

Asian cooks often use water chestnut flour in batters and puddings and as a thickener in sauces. Using it along with flour in a batter gives fried foods a crisper and lighter crust. Look for it in Asian food stores. Stored in a covered container it will keep for a few weeks.

YELLOW BEAN SAUCE (see Bean Sauces, page 28)

INGREDIENT TRANSLATION CHART
A Shopper's Guide

ENGLISH	CHINESE	INDONESIAN	MALAY	OTHER
Bean Curd, Deep-Fried	dou fu pok	tahu goreng	tahu	
Bean Curd, Fresh	dou fu	tahu	tahu	
Bean Curd Sheets or Sticks, Dried	(dou) fu juk			
Bean (Soybean) Sauces	min sze jeung		tau cheo	
Bitter Melon	foo gwa		peria	
Black Peppercorns		lada hitam *or* merica	lada hitam *or* merica	
Candlenuts		kemiri	buah keras	
Cardamom		kapulaga	buah pelaga	
Chiles, Fresh	laat jiu	lombok hijau	cabai	sabz mirich (Hindi)
Chiles, Dried		lombok	cabai	prik chee (Thai) lal mirich (Hindi)
Cinnamon		kayu manis	kayu manis	darchini (Hindi)
Cloves		bunga cengkeh	cengkeh	laung (Hindi)
Coconut Milk and Coconut Cream		santen *or* santen kental (thick)	santen	kathi (Thai)
Coriander, Fresh	yuen sai	daun ketumbar	daun ketumbar	dhania (Hindi)
Coriander Seeds		ketumbar	ketumbar	
Cumin Seeds		jinten	jintan puteh	
Curry or Kari Leaves			daun kari	meetha neem (Hindi)
Dried Black Mushrooms	doon gwoo			
Dried Shrimp	ha mai	udang kering	udang kering	
Fennel Seeds		adas	jintan manis	sonf (Hindi)
Five-Spice Powder	ng heung fun		serbuk lima rempah	

ENGLISH	CHINESE	INDONESIAN	MALAY	OTHER
Galangal (see Siamese Ginger)		laos, lengkuas	lengkuas	kha (Thai)
Ginger	geung	djane	halia	adrak (Hindi)
Glutinous (Sweet) Rice	naw mai	ketan	pulot	
Kaffir Lime Leaves		djeruk perut	daun limau perut	bai makrut (Thai)
Lemongrass		sereh	serai	sera (Hindi)
Lily Buds, Dried	gum jum			
Mung Bean Thread Noodles	fun see		sohoon *or* tunghoon	
Pandan Leaves			daun pandan	bai toey (Thai)
Plum Sauce	suen muey jeung			
Polygonum or Laksa Leaves			daun kesom	
Shrimp Paste, Dried (fermented)		terasi	blachan *or* belacan	kapi (Thai)
Siamese Ginger or Greater Galangal		laos	lengkuas	kha (Thai)
Star Anise	bot gok	bunga lawang	bunga lawang	
Tamarind		asam	asam	som ma kham (Thai)
Thick Shrimp Paste			petis	
Turmeric	wong heung fun	kunyit	kunyit	haldi (Hindi)

APPETIZERS AND SOUPS

"Top Hats" (*Kway Pai Ti*)
Fried Bean Curd Salad
with Spicy Peanut Dressing
(*Tahu Goreng*)
Savory Vegetable-Filled Pastries
(*Samosas*)
Mixed Vegetables
with Peanut Sauce (*Gado Gado*)
Raw Fish Salad
with Crisp Shredded Vegetables
(*Yu Sang*)
Fresh Vegetable Spring Rolls
(*Poh Pia*)
Grilled Beef on Skewers (*Satay*)
Pork Rib Tea Soup (*Bak Ku Teh*)
Lamb Soup (*Soup Kambing*)
Spicy Chicken Soup
with Potato Fritters (*Soto Ayam*)
Lentil Vegetable Soup (*Dalca*)

Clockwise from left: Satay (page 60), Kway Pai Ti (page 48), Poh Pia (page 58), Samosas (page 52)

KWAY PAI TI
"Top Hats"
(*Nonya*)

These dainty, crisp pastry shells filled with shrimp and shredded vegetables make an exotic hors d'oeuvre for the buffet table or to be passed on a tray. They are one of the most popular appetizers at the Straits Cafe. To make the shells you need special cast-iron molds shaped like inverted top hats without rims; one will do, but with a few you can fry several "top hats" at once.

You can buy similar pre-made shells at many import and foreign specialty food stores. A 2-inch-wide metal pastry mold will make a crimped top hat, but it needs to be held with long-handled tongs during frying, so you have to be very careful. Although it won't taste quite as good, you can also shape and deep-fry commercially made won ton wrappers (see Note at end of recipe).

Makes 30

PASTRY SHELLS
1½ cups all-purpose flour
½ cup rice flour
1 teaspoon salt
1 small egg
1½ cups water
Vegetable oil for deep-frying

FILLING
2 tablespoons vegetable oil
1 teaspoon chopped garlic
2 ounces medium shrimp (41 to 50 per pound), shelled, deveined, and cut into ¼-inch dice
1½ teaspoons dried shrimp, chopped
3 ounces canned bamboo shoot strips (about ¾ cup)
1½ cups julienne carrots, ⅛ inch thick by 2 inches long; about 2 carrots, peeled
2 cups julienne jicama, ⅛ inch thick by 2 inches long; about 6 ounces, peeled (see Note)
2 cups water
1 tablespoon sugar
1 teaspoon salt

✿

Sweet Chile Sauce (see page 162), for topping
Fresh coriander leaves, for garnish

1. **To make the pastry shells,** sift both flours and the salt into a mixing bowl. Add the egg and water and mix thoroughly. The batter should have the consistency of thin pancake batter.

2. Pour 3 inches of oil into a deep saucepan. Heat the oil to 365°F. Dip a pastry shell mold

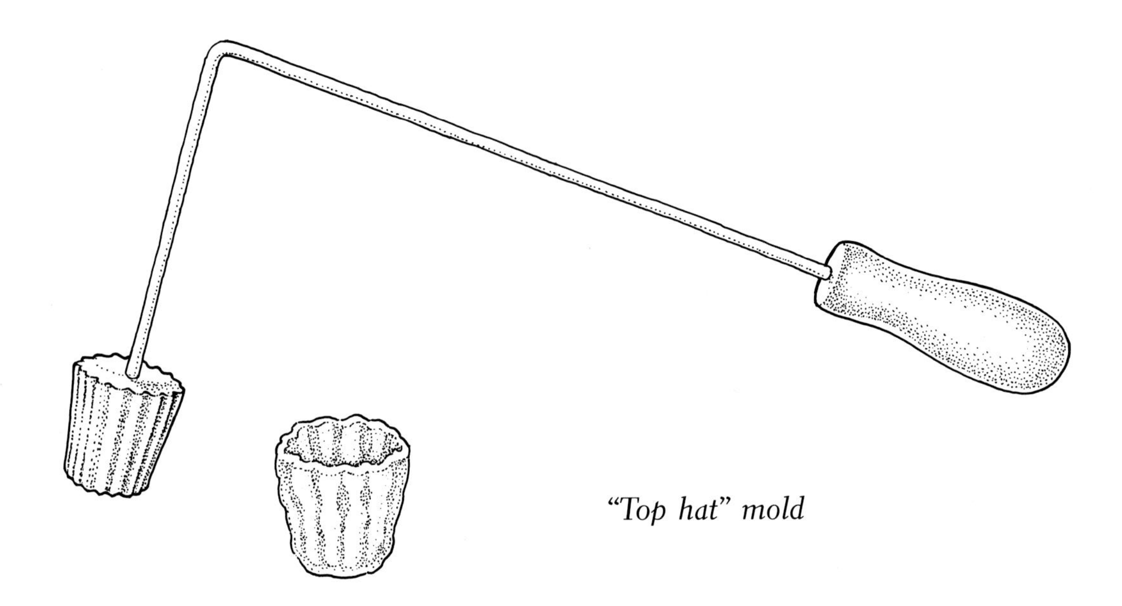

"Top hat" mold

into the oil for a few seconds, then dip the mold into the batter up to the top edge, but not over the top. Carefully place the batter-covered mold into the hot oil; deep-fry for about 1 minute. With chopsticks or tongs, nudge the top edge of the shell to loosen it from the mold. Continue frying until the cup turns golden brown, about 1 minute longer. Remove the shell and drain it on paper towels. Dip the mold again, first in the oil then in the batter, and fry the next shell. There should be enough batter for 30 shells. The shells can be made a day ahead; store them in a single layer in an airtight container.

3. **To make the filling,** heat 2 tablespoons of oil in a large saucepan. Add the garlic, shrimp, dried shrimp, bamboo shoots, carrots, and jicama; saute until the shrimp turn bright pink. Add the water, sugar, and salt and bring the mixture to a boil. Reduce the heat and simmer until the vegetables are tender and just enough liquid is left to keep the mixture moist, about 20 minutes; let cool.

4. **To serve,** fill the pastry cups with filling and top each with a few drops of Sweet Chili Sauce and a fresh coriander leaf. Fill the shells just before serving.

NOTE: To make a pastry shell from a won ton wrapper, carefully lower a fresh wrapper into the hot oil and immediately depress the center with a small stainless steel ladle (about 1½ inches wide). Deep-fry for about 10 seconds, remove the ladle, and deep-fry for a few seconds longer or until golden brown. Remove and drain.

NOTE: Jicama is a brown-skinned root vegetable called "yam bean" in Singapore. It was introduced into the Philippines by the Spanish in the 17th century.

TAHU GORENG

Fried Bean Curd Salad with Spicy Peanut Dressing
(*Indonesian*)

This "salad" provides a delicious contrast to the Western concept of salad. Beneath the spicy and sweet peanut dressing lie the crispy skin and creamy-smooth, cool interior of deep-fried tofu.

Serves 4 to 6

DRESSING
1 teaspoon (2 cloves) garlic
2 teaspoons dark soy sauce
½ cup tamarind water (see page 41)
3 tablespoons ground roasted peanuts
3 tablespoons sugar
½ teaspoon sriracha sauce
1 teaspoon lemon juice

✿

2 ounces fresh bean sprouts
2 squares fresh firm tofu (each about 2½ inches square by 1 inch thick)
Vegetable oil for deep-frying
Finely shredded carrots, for garnish
Thin cucumber slices, for garnish

1. **To prepare the dressing,** mash the garlic in a garlic press. Combine with the soy sauce, tamarind water, peanuts, sugar, sriracha sauce, and lemon juice; blend thoroughly. Set aside.

2. Blanch the bean sprouts in boiling water until they begin to wilt, about 5 seconds. Drain. Rinse with cold water. Drain well.

3. Pat the tofu thoroughly dry with paper towels. Preheat a wok or saucepan and add oil to a depth of 2 inches; heat the oil to 365°F. Carefully lower the tofu into the oil and deep-fry until golden brown, about 4 to 5 minutes. Remove and drain. Cut each tofu square in half and then into thirds crosswise. Arrange the pieces on a serving plate. Scatter the bean sprouts over the tofu and pour the dressing on top. Garnish with shredded carrots and cucumber slices. Serve immediately.

SAMOSAS

Savory Vegetable-Filled Pastries
(*Indian*)

Samosas, a traditional snack food in India, are delightful puffy triangles filled with a blend of vegetables, spices, and herbs. They simply melt in your mouth. This version uses Chinese spring roll wrappers in place of the traditional pastry dough, an obvious Singaporean adaptation. You may also substitute commercially prepared lumpia wrappers.

Makes about 4 dozen

4 large potatoes
3 onions
10 cloves garlic, peeled
1-inch chunk fresh ginger, peeled
2 tablespoons vegetable oil
2 tablespoons fresh or frozen curry leaves, if available
2 to 3 tablespoons Red Chile Paste (see page 39) or 3 fresh serrano chiles, chopped
2 tablespoons curry powder (yellow Indian style)
½ cup peas, blanched
½ cup blanched carrots, in ¼-inch dice
1½ teaspoons salt
1 tablespoon sugar
3 tablespoons flour
2 packages spring roll wrappers (Menlo brand) or lumpia wrappers, approximately 8½ inches square
Vegetable oil for deep-frying
Sweet Chile Sauce (see page 162) or commercially prepared Chinese plum sauce

1. Boil the potatoes until tender. When cool, peel and cut them into ¼-inch dice. Set aside.

2. Peel the onions. Cut 2 into 1-inch chunks. Put the chunks into a food processor with the garlic and ginger; puree. If you prefer using a blender, add just enough water to facilitate the blending. Finely chop and set aside the remaining onion.

3. Preheat a wok and add the oil, onion-ginger mixture, and curry leaves. Saute over low heat for 3 to 5 minutes or until thick. Add the red chile paste and chopped onion; saute a minute longer until syrupy. Add the curry powder, potatoes, peas, and carrots; mix together over low heat. Season with salt and sugar. Increase the heat and cook, stirring, to reduce the liquids. The filling should have a dry consistency. Transfer it to a plate and allow it to cool. You should have about 6 cups of filling.

4. Mix the flour with enough water to make a thin paste. Cut one spring roll wrapper in half diagonally to make two triangles. Set one triangle down with the 90 degree angle toward you. Put about 2 teaspoons of filling in the middle. Fold the left-hand corner over to the middle of

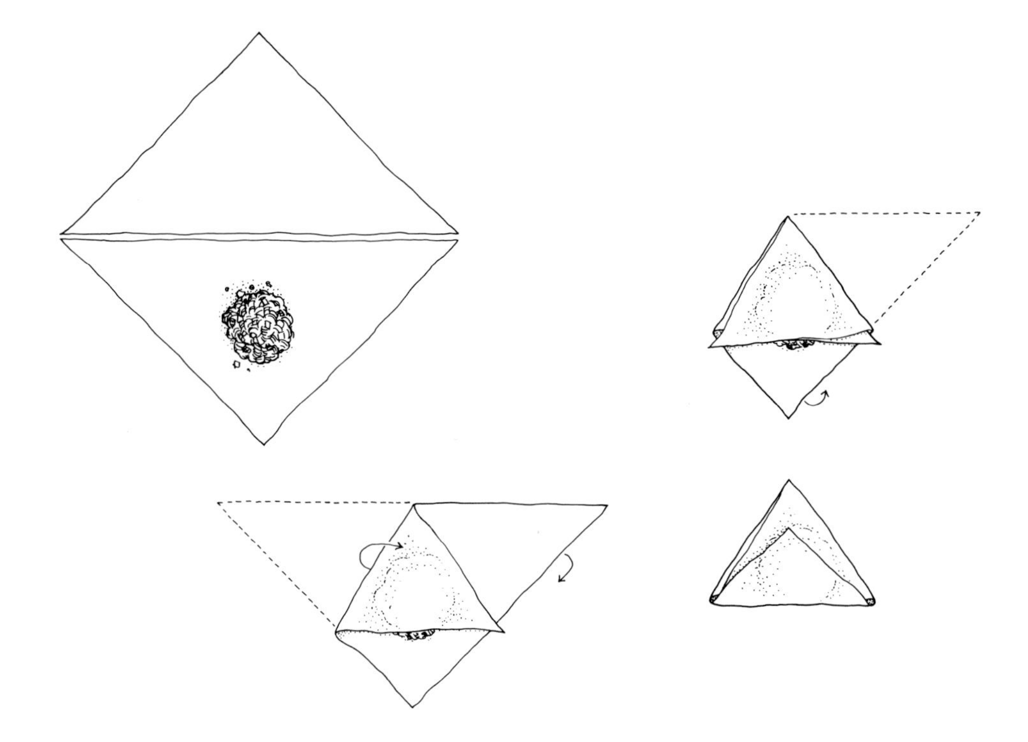

the opposite edge. Fold the right corner over to its opposite edge, enclosing the filling. Fold up the lower corner. Seal the edges with flour paste. Repeat with the remaining wrappers and filling. Freeze any leftover wrappers.

5. Preheat a wok and add oil to a depth of 2 inches. Heat the oil to 365°F. Carefully lower a few triangles into the hot oil and deep-fry for 1 minute, or until they turn golden brown. Remove and drain on paper towels. When all the triangles are fried, serve them with sweet chile sauce.

GADO GADO

Mixed Vegetables with Peanut Sauce

(*Indonesian*)

This popular salad is the Southeast Asian version of crudités, with a piquant peanut dressing and a topping of fried *krupuk* chips that gives it extra crunch.

Serves 4

2 cups blanched bean sprouts
2 cups blanched cabbage, cut into 1½-inch cubes
2 cups blanched long green beans, cut into 2-inch lengths

REMPAH
5 quarter-size slices fresh galangal, cut up (see Note)
5 candlenuts, soaked in water for 10 minutes, or skinless almonds
5 stalks fresh lemongrass, trimmed and sliced
10 shallots (walnut-size) or 2 large onions, peeled and sliced
6 cloves garlic, peeled and sliced
1 teaspoon turmeric powder
1 cup vegetable oil
3 tablespoons Red Chile Paste (see page 39)

✿

1 can (13½ ounces) unsweetened coconut milk, shaken well
5 tablespoons sugar
1½ teaspoons salt
2 cups ground roasted peanuts
4 cups cold boiled potatoes, peeled and cut into 1½-inch cubes
1 cucumber, peeled and cut into ½-inch cubes
4 squares deep-fried bean curd, each cut into 4 pieces (see page 166)
4 hard-cooked eggs, peeled and cut into wedges
20 fried *krupuk* chips (see page 168)

1. Blot the blanched vegetables dry. Cover and refrigerate them until ready to serve.

2. To prepare the *rempah*, grind the galangal, candlenuts, lemongrass, shallots, garlic, and turmeric to a smooth paste in a blender or food processor. Add a tablespoon or more of water if needed to facilitate the blending. Heat a wok over low heat. Add the oil and chile paste and fry, stirring frequently, until the oil takes on a red hue, about 2 minutes. Add the ground ingredients and fry, stirring frequently, until they are completely combined with the oil. Continue frying and stirring until the *rempah* is fragrant and has a porridge-like consistency, about 10 minutes. It is done when oil seeps out.

3. Add the coconut milk, sugar, salt, and peanuts; simmer over low heat until oil separates from

the sauce, about 10 minutes. Transfer the sauce to a bowl and allow it to cool.

4. Neatly arrange the bean sprouts, cabbage, green beans, potatoes, cucumber, fried bean curd, and eggs on a large serving platter or divide them among 4 individual salad plates. Pour the sauce over and garnish with the *krupuk* chips.

NOTE: You can substitute dried galangal for fresh. Use half as much as called for in the recipe. Soak the dried galangal in water for 1 hour, then cut it into smaller pieces.

YU SANG

Raw Fish Salad with Crisp Shredded Vegetables (*Chinese/Malay*)

Yu Sang is a treat for sashimi lovers. The Chinese living in Malaysia and Singapore have made a tradition of serving it during Chinese New Year. The combination of shredded carrots, Chinese radish (*daikon*), pickled shallots, two kinds of shredded ginger, and raw fish in a sweet-sour plum sauce dressing is refreshing and distinctively Malaysianized Chinese food.

Ikan parang (wolf herring) is the preferred fish for this dish because of its delicate taste, but it is bony. Jenny Fong, executive chef at the Straits Cafe and a Nonya from Malaysia, explains that cooks there deal with the tiny bones by cutting the fish across the grain into very thin slices. The slices contain minuscule flecks of bone which can be eaten. At the Straits Cafe this salad is made with raw tuna, which is what we recommend. If using another type of fish, pluck out the bones with needle-nose pliers. A mandoline or food processor makes the very fine shredding of the radish and carrot a breeze.

Serves 4 to 6

¼ pound very fresh tuna (about 6 × 2 × ½ inches)
2 cups finely shredded Chinese white radish (*daikon*)
2 cups finely shredded carrot

DRESSING
⅔ cup bottled plum sauce (see page 38)
½ cup water
1 tablespoon vegetable oil
⅓ cup sugar
Salt to taste

MARINADE
1 teaspoon vegetable oil
1 teaspoon Asian sesame oil
¼ teaspoon sugar
⅛ teaspoon salt
⅛ teaspoon white pepper
⅛ teaspoon five-spice powder
Juice of ½ lemon

✿

1-inch chunk fresh ginger, preferably young ginger, shredded paper thin
⅓ cup finely shredded sweet pickled ginger (bottled)
8 pickled shallots, finely shredded (about ⅓ cup)
7 fresh or frozen kaffir lime leaves (see page 31), finely shredded with scissors
1 large red jalapeño chile, seeded and finely shredded
2 green onions, green part only, finely shredded
¼ bunch fresh coriander, leaves only
¼ cup chopped peanuts
Toasted sesame seeds, for garnish
Chinese shrimp chips, for garnish (see *krupuk*, page 168)

1. Remove any bones from the fish. Freeze it until firm, then cut it across the grain into paper-thin slices, about 2 inches long. Set aside in the refrigerator.

2. In separate bowls, cover the finely shredded radish and carrots with cold water; set aside while you prepare the other ingredients.

3. To make the dressing, mix the plum sauce and water together; strain into a bowl. Heat the oil in a wok or saucepan over low heat; add the plum sauce, sugar, and salt. Cook until the sugar dissolves. Cool.

4. Mix the marinade ingredients together in a medium bowl. Add the fish slices and toss. Mound the fish in the center of a platter.

5. Rinse the carrots and radish and squeeze out the excess water. Surround the fish with radish and carrot shreds. Scatter the two gingers, shallots, lime leaves, chile, green onions, and coriander leaves over the fish. Top with peanuts and sesame seeds. Spoon half of the dressing over the salad. It is customary for everyone to join in and help toss the salad with their chopsticks by digging to the bottom and tossing up and over. When the salad is fully tossed, add the remaining dressing and serve on individual salad plates. Garnish with shrimp chips.

POH PIA

Fresh Vegetable Spring Rolls

(*Nonya*)

Poh Pia, Straits Chinese-style spring rolls, are served "fresh," meaning the wrappers are not fried, so they are light and refreshing. The shrimp and vegetable filling is the same as is used for *Kway Pai Ti,* "Top Hats" (page 48).

Don't let the long list of ingredients discourage you. *Poh Pia* is an ideal buffet luncheon dish. You can simply set out all the ingredients and sauces on the buffet table and let your guests assemble spring rolls to their taste.

Makes about 15

FILLING
2 tablespoons vegetable oil
1 teaspoon chopped garlic
2 ounces medium shrimp (41 to 50 per pound), shelled, deveined, and cut into ¼-inch dice
1½ teaspoons dried shrimp, chopped
3 ounces canned bamboo shoot strips (about ¾ cup)
1½ cups julienne carrots, ⅛ inch thick by 2 inches long; about 2 carrots, peeled
2 cups julienne jicama, ⅛ inch thick by 2 inches long; about 6 ounces, peeled (see Note, page 49)
2 cups water
1 tablespoon sugar
1 teaspoon salt

✿

1 package spring roll wrappers (Menlo brand)
¾ cup hoisin sauce
3 tablespoons sriracha sauce, or more to taste
3 Chinese sausages, steamed and coarsely chopped
4 eggs, cooked into 2 thin omelettes and cut into ¼-inch-wide strips
30 cooked medium shrimp (41 to 50 per pound), cut in half lengthwise
Sprigs of fresh coriander, for garnish

1. **To make the filling,** heat the oil in a large saucepan. Add the garlic, shrimp, dried shrimp, bamboo shoots, carrots, and jicama and saute until the shrimp turn bright pink. Add the water, sugar, and salt and bring the mixture to a boil. Reduce the heat and simmer until the vegetables are tender and just enough liquid is left to keep the mixture moist, about 20 minutes. Set aside to cool.

2. **To assemble,** lay a spring roll wrapper down with one corner toward you. Cut another wrapper into 3 equal strips (you will need 4 wrappers for each 3 spring rolls). Place one of the strips

horizontally across the middle of the wrapper. Smear about 2 teaspoons of hoisin sauce over the middle strip. Add ½ to 1 teaspoon of sriracha sauce (depending on how much heat you like). Spread about ⅓ cup of the vegetable filling over the sauces and scatter some Chinese sausage, egg strips, and 3 or 4 shrimp halves on top. Fold the bottom edge of the wrapper up over the filling. Tuck in the side corners and roll up the spring roll. Repeat with the remaining wrappers and filling.

3. **To serve,** you can slice each spring roll into 4 or 5 pieces or serve them whole. Garnish with a swirl of hoisin sauce and sriracha sauce and a sprig of fresh coriander.

SATAY

Grilled Beef on Skewers
(*Malay*)

Satay originated in Indonesia and is now popular throughout Southeast Asia. The many variations in the marinade and peanut sauce reflect the influences of local ethnic cooks. The most common and popular satays are made with barbecued or grilled beef, lamb, chicken, or seafood. Pork is used only on the island of Bali, where the majority of the population is Hindu rather than Muslim. The satay served at the Straits Cafe has a mildly seasoned marinade and a peanut sauce that is sweet and full of exotic flavors.

Makes 15

MARINADE
1½ teaspoons whole fennel seeds
1½ teaspoons whole cumin seeds
2 quarter-size slices fresh galangal, chopped (see **Note, page 55**)
1 stalk fresh lemongrass, trimmed and sliced
5 shallots (walnut-size) or 1 large onion, peeled and sliced
4 cloves garlic, peeled and sliced
1 tablespoon ground coriander
1 teaspoon turmeric powder
2 tablespoons sugar
¼ teaspoon salt

✿

1 pound beef chuck
15 bamboo skewers
Satay Sauce (**page 158**)

1. **To prepare the marinade,** heat a dry skillet or wok and lightly toast the fennel and cumin seeds. When cool grind them in a spice mill and set aside. Grind the galangal, lemongrass, shallots, garlic, coriander, and turmeric to a smooth paste in a blender or food processor. If necessary, add 1 or more tablespoons of water to facilitate the blending. Transfer the paste to a bowl and mix in the ground seeds, sugar, and salt.

2. Cut the beef lengthwise (across the grain) into ¼-inch-thick slices, then crosswise into 1-inch pieces. Add the beef to the marinade, mix together, and marinate in the refrigerator for at least 30 minutes, or preferably overnight.

3. Soak the bamboo skewers in a pan of water for at least 1 hour. Thread 3 pieces of beef onto each skewer. If you are not going to cook the satay right away, refrigerate the skewered meat.

4. Place the skewers on a pre-heated grill 4 to 6 inches above hot glowing charcoal or under the broiler. Grill about 1 minute on each side or until the meat is seared. Serve with Satay Sauce for dipping.

BAK KU TEH

Pork Rib Tea Soup
(*Chinese—Hokkien*)

In Singapore breakfast often consists of a bowl of pork rib tea soup, a strip of deep-fried cruller, and, instead of coffee, a minuscule pot of strong black tea. The soup is light and thin, yet it exudes delicious herbal and spicy aromas. The cruller is a baguette-shaped Chinese savory doughnut, similar to a French *beignet,* meant to be dunked into the aromatic soup. Pick some up next time you are shopping in an Asian market.

Serves 4 to 6

1 pound pork spareribs (see Note)
5 cloves garlic, peeled
1 thumb-size piece *tung kwai* (optional, see Note)
2½ quarts water
3 cinnamon sticks
5 whole star anise or broken pieces equal to 5 stars
1 tablespoon white peppercorns
1 tablespoon black peppercorns
2 teaspoons salt
2 teaspoons sugar
1 tablespoon dark soy sauce, or to taste
2 tablespoons Crisp Shallot Flakes (page 166)
Soy sauce with thinly sliced red chiles, for dipping
Steamed white rice
2 Chinese crullers, sliced diagonally (optional)

Place the sparerib pieces in a large pot and add enough cold water to cover them. Parboil until scum rises to the surface. Drain and rinse the meat with cold water and return it to the pot. Add the garlic, *tung kwai,* and 2½ quarts of water. Wrap the cinnamon, star anise, and peppercorns in cheesecloth; tie it and add the bag to the pot. Bring the water to a boil, reduce the heat, and simmer uncovered for 1 hour or until the meat shrinks from the bones. Skim the excess oil from the surface and discard. Remove the spice bag. Season the soup with salt, sugar, and dark soy sauce to taste. Serve with 3 to 4 sparerib pieces per serving. Scatter 1 teaspoon of Crisp Shallot Flakes over each serving. Dip the ribs into soy sauce with chiles and eat them with steamed rice. Dunk the cruller slices into the broth and enjoy.

NOTE: When you buy the spareribs, have your butcher chop them into 1½-inch pieces across the bones.

NOTE: *Tung kwai* is a medicinal root available in herbal shops and better Asian food markets.

SOUP KAMBING

Lamb Soup

(*Indian*)

This soup is light but rich with the hearty flavors of Indian spices. It was originally made with mutton, because that was the available meat in India. In Singapore and Malaysia the soup is garnished with crisp fried shallots and served with chunks of French bread.

Serves 6

5 cloves garlic, peeled
3-inch chunk peeled ginger, cut into ½-inch pieces
½ onion, cut into chunks
1 tablespoon whole cardamom pods
1 tablespoon ground fennel seeds
1 tablespoon ground cumin seeds
1 tablespoon ground coriander
½ tablespoon whole cloves
3 sticks cinnamon
1½ pounds leg of lamb, left whole
3 quarts water
2 tablespoons dark soy sauce
1 ounce Chinese celery (or regular celery), cut into 2-inch lengths
2 tomatoes, cut into quarters and then crosswise in half
1 teaspoon Indian-style curry powder (optional)
3 tablespoons cornstarch dissolved in ½ cup water
Crisp Shallot Flakes, for garnish (page 166)
Chopped Chinese celery leaves, for garnish
French bread

Puree the garlic, ginger, and onion in a food processor or blender. Transfer the puree to a stock pot. Tie the cardamom, fennel, cumin, coriander, cloves, and cinnamon in a piece of fine mesh cotton cheesecloth. Add the spice bag to the stockpot. Add the lamb, water, and soy sauce; bring to a boil. Reduce the heat and simmer uncovered for 30 minutes. Add the celery and tomatoes and simmer 1 hour longer. Remove the lamb from the pot; discard the spice bag and strain the stock. When the meat has cooled, remove it from the bone, cut it into ½-inch pieces, and add it back to the stock. Stir in the curry powder. Bring the soup to a boil. Add the cornstarch liquid and stir continuously until the soup thickens to a thin cream consistency. Garnish each serving with a sprinkling of Crisp Shallot Flakes and celery leaves. Serve with crusty French bread.

SOTO AYAM

Spicy Chicken Soup with Potato Fritters
(*Malay/Indonesian*)

Many Singaporean dishes are quite simple; it is the array of garnishes that accompanies the dish that makes it so exciting and interesting. A perfect example is *Soto Ayam*, a popular street-hawker and family-style soup. It is a simple chicken soup spiked with mild seasonings. The accompanying garnishes add dimension, complementing the soup and stimulating the palate. Make as many or as few garnishes as you like, and set the table so that your guests can garnish their own soup.

Serves 6

REMPAH
2 quarter-size slices fresh galangal, cut up (see Note, page 55)
8 shallots (walnut-size) or 2 onions, peeled and sliced
1-inch chunk fresh ginger, peeled and sliced
5 cloves garlic, peeled and sliced

✿

3½ quarts water
1 chicken (2½ pounds)
2 stalks fresh lemongrass, trimmed and slapped with the side of a cleaver or bruised with a mallet
2 teaspoons cumin seeds
2 teaspoons fennel seeds
2½ tablespoons ground coriander
2 teaspoons whole cardamom pods
2 sticks cinnamon
1 tablespoon sugar
1½ teaspoons salt

GARNISHES
6 cups fresh bean sprouts
***Lontong* (page 81), cut into 1-inch cubes**
Potato Perkedel (page 167)
6 tablespoons chopped Chinese celery or parsley
3 tablespoons Crisp Shallot Flakes (page 166)

1. To prepare the *rempah,* grind the galangal, shallots, ginger, and garlic to a smooth paste in a blender or food processor. Add a tablespoon or more of water if needed to facilitate the blending. Transfer the mixture to a stockpot.

2. Add the water, chicken, and lemongrass to the pot and bring it to a boil. Skim and discard the scum from the surface; reduce to a simmer. Grind the cumin and fennel seeds to a powder

in a spice mill. Put them in a fine-mesh muslin cloth spice bag with the coriander, cardamom, and cinnamon; add the bag to the stockpot. Simmer for 45 minutes.

3. Season the soup with sugar and salt. Remove the chicken, discard the spice bag and the lemongrass. Strain the stock and keep it warm (you should have about 10 cups). When the chicken is cool, hand tear the meat into shreds.

4. To serve, put 1 cup of bean sprouts in each soup bowl. Scatter ½ cup of shredded chicken, 3 *lontong* cubes, and 1 potato perkedel on top. Pour about 1½ cups of hot chicken stock over the garnishes. Top with Chinese celery and shallot flakes.

DALCA

Lentil Vegetable Soup

(*North Indian/Singaporean*)

This soup is hearty vegetarian fare which can easily serve as a meal in itself. It is a complex marriage of sweet, sour, and savory flavors, with a strong infusion of exotic spices mellowed by coconut milk. The recipe was originated by Chef Wan Ismail at the Straits Cafe.

Serves 4 to 6

⅓ cup yellow lentils (*toovar dal*)

SPICE BOUQUET
2 sticks cinnamon
1 teaspoon whole cardamom pods
½ teaspoon whole cloves
4 whole star anise

REMPAH
1-inch chunk fresh ginger, peeled and sliced
4 shallots (walnut-size) or 1 medium onion, peeled and sliced
4 cloves garlic, peeled and sliced
3 fresh red jalapeño chiles, seeded, stems removed
¼ cup ghee or vegetable oil
1 tablespoon curry powder

✿

1 cup tamarind water (see page 41)
1 can (13½ ounces) unsweetened coconut milk
1 cup water

1 carrot, peeled and cut into ¼-inch pieces
¼ head cauliflower, trimmed and broken into bite-size florets
1 Asian eggplant, quartered lengthwise and cut into 2-inch lengths
1 cup Chinese long beans or common green beans, cut into 1-inch lengths
1 large boiled potato, peeled and cut into ½-inch cubes
1 tablespoon sugar
½ teaspoon salt

1. Sort through the lentils, discarding any that are cracked or shrivelled and any pebbles. Wash and drain the lentils. Cover them with water and gently boil until they are tender but firm, about 20 minutes. Drain. Tie the ingredients for the spice bouquet in cheesecloth.

2. To make the *rempah,* grind the ginger, shallots, garlic, and chiles to a smooth paste in a blender or food processor. Add a tablespoon or more of water if needed to facilitate the blending. Heat the ghee in a wok or saucepan over low heat. Add the ground mixture and fry, stirring frequently, until the *rempah* is fragrant and has a creamy, porridge-like consistency, about 8 to 10 minutes. Stir in the curry powder. Transfer the *rempah* to a large saucepan.

3. Add the tamarind water, drained lentils, coconut milk, water, and the spice bouquet; bring to a boil. Add the carrot and cauliflower, reduce the heat, and cook at a low boil for 5 minutes. Add the eggplant and beans and cook 3 minutes longer. Add the potato and season with the sugar and salt; cook 1 minute longer. Remove the spice bouquet. Serve hot with *Roti Prata* (page 86) or other hearty bread.

NOODLES, RICE, AND BREADS

Noodles with Chicken and Mushrooms (*Gai See Mee*)
Fresh Rice "Spaghetti" Noodles in Spicy Coconut Gravy (*Laksa Lemak*)
Fried Noodles Indian Style (*Mee Goreng*)
Prawn Two-Noodle Soup (*Hay Mee*)
Rice Noodles in a Tangy Gravy with Seafood (*Mee Siam*)
Dry-Style Noodles with Lemon and Toasted Coconut (*Mee Karabu*)
Stir-Fried Rice Noodles with Shrimp and Chinese Sausage (*Chow Kway Teo*)
Rice Noodles Stir-Fried with Seafood (*Hokkien Bee Hoon*)
Rice Cooked in Banana Leaves (*Lontong*)
Malaysian-Style Fried Rice (*Nasi Goreng*)
Fragrant Rice Simmered in Coconut Milk (*Nasi Lemak*)
Turmeric Rice with Coconut Milk (*Nasi Kunyit*)
Indian Fry Bread
Indian Griddled Bread (*Roti Prata*)
Spicy Meat-Stuffed Griddled Bread (*Murtabak*)

Laksa Lemak (page 71)

GAI SEE MEE

Noodles with Chicken and Mushrooms
(*Chinese*)

In this quick and easy noodle dish a lightly thickened sauce generously coats the boiled noodles. It makes a wonderful lunch entree.

Serves 3 to 4

6 Chinese dried black mushrooms
3 cups chicken stock
3 tablespoons oyster sauce
3 tablespoons rice wine
1 tablespoon dark soy sauce
1½ tablespoons sugar
2½ tablespoons cornstarch mixed with ⅓ cup water
1 pound Chinese thin egg noodles
Asian sesame oil, to taste
1 cup shredded poached chicken
Chopped green onions, for garnish
Crisp Shallot Flakes (page 166)

1. Cover the mushrooms with warm water until soft and pliable, about 30 minutes. Drain and squeeze out the excess water. Cut off the stems at the base and discard. Cut the caps into thin slices.

2. Combine the stock, oyster sauce, rice wine, soy sauce, sugar, and mushrooms in a wok or saucepan. Bring to a boil. Reduce the heat and simmer for 5 minutes. Return to a boil. Stir in the cornstarch mixture and cook, stirring, until the mixture thickens to a thin creamy consistency. Keep warm.

3. Bring 2 to 3 quarts of water to a boil. Add the noodles. Bring to a second boil and boil 1 minute. Drain the noodles in a colander and rinse them well with cold water. Shake off the excess water.

4. To serve, reheat the noodles by dropping them into a pot of boiling water for a few seconds. Drain well. Divide the noodles among 3 or 4 individual plates. Dribble a bit of sesame oil over the noodles, evenly distribute the chicken, and pour the hot sauce (with the mushrooms) over all. Garnish with green onions and Crisp Shallot Flakes. Serve hot.

LAKSA LEMAK

Fresh Rice "Spaghetti" Noodles in Spicy Coconut Gravy (*Nonya*)

Laksa, fresh rice "spaghetti" noodles, are served in two styles in Singapore. Penang-style *laksa* has a thin mackerel-based gravy and the sour taste of tamarind; this Nonya version has a rich soup made with coconut milk. Dried rice noodles (*bee hoon*) may be substituted.

Serves 4

REMPAH
1/3 cup dried shrimp, soaked in water for 10 minutes and drained
6 candlenuts, soaked in water for 10 minutes and drained, or skinless almonds
4 stalks fresh lemongrass, trimmed and sliced
12 shallots (walnut-size) or 2 large onions, peeled and halved
6 cloves garlic, peeled and halved
1 1/2 teaspoons turmeric powder
1 teaspoon *blachan* (dried shrimp paste)
1/3 cup vegetable oil
3 tablespoons Red Chile Paste (see page 39)

✿

1 can (13 1/2 ounces) unsweetened coconut milk plus 1 can water
4 teaspoons sugar
1 1/2 teaspoons salt
1 1/2 pounds *laksa* noodles
2 cups blanched bean sprouts
24 1/4-inch-thick slices fried fish cake (see Note, page 81)
16 cooked large shrimp or 1 cup poached shredded chicken breast
1 tablespoon chopped laksa leaf (*daun kesom*)

1. To make the *rempah,* grind the dried shrimp, candlenuts, lemongrass, shallots, garlic, turmeric, and *blachan* to a smooth paste in a blender or food processor. Add a tablespoon or more of water if needed to facilitate the blending. Heat the oil in a wok or saucepan and add the chile paste. Fry, stirring continuously, until the oil takes on a reddish hue, about 2 minutes. Add the ground mixture and fry over low heat, stirring frequently, until it is completely combined with the oil. Continue frying and stirring for 5 to 8 minutes until the *rempah* is fragrant and has a deep mahogany-red color and porridge-like consistency. It is ready when reddish oil seeps out.

2. Add the coconut milk and water and bring to a boil. Reduce the heat, season with sugar and salt, and simmer 10 minutes. You should have about 5 cups of soup gravy.

3. Scald the noodles in boiling water for 1 minute. Drain. Rinse with cold water; drain. Divide the noodles and then the bean sprouts among 4 deep bowls. Pour in the soup gravy. Top each bowl with a few fish cake slices, shrimp or chicken, and some laksa leaf.

MEE GORENG

Fried Noodles Indian Style

(*Malay/Indian*)

A popular hawker food, *Mee Goreng* is an Indian-style fried noodle dish loaded with garlic, tomatoes, potatoes, cabbage, and shrimp. The Indian cooks in Malaysia and Singapore are famous for their *Mee Goreng,* but you would never find this dish in India. Although it is prepared in Singapore with thick yellow Hokkien-style noodles, the medium-width or flat Chinese egg noodles available in better American supermarkets substitute quite well.

Serves 2 to 4 as a light meal

½ pound Chinese egg noodles
2 tablespoons vegetable oil
2 teaspoons chopped garlic
¼ pound medium shrimp (41 to 50 per pound), shelled, deveined, and split in half lengthwise
1 cup cabbage cut into ¾-inch cubes
1 tomato, cut into ½-inch cubes
1-inch square deep-fried tofu, cut into ¼-inch-thick slices
1 medium boiled potato, cut into ¾-inch cubes
½ teaspoon salt
1 teaspoon sugar
2 tablespoons tomato ketchup
1 teaspoon sriracha sauce or Red Chile Paste (see page 39)
2 eggs
¼ pound bean sprouts (about 2 handfuls)
Sliced jalapeño chiles, for garnish
Fresh Chinese celery leaves, for garnish
Crisp Shallot Flakes (page 166)
Lemon wedges, for garnish

1. Bring 2 to 3 quarts of water to a boil. Add the noodles. Bring to a second boil, then boil 1 minute longer. Drain the noodles in a colander. Rinse well with cold water, shake off any excess water, and set aside.

2. Preheat a wok over medium heat. When hot, add the oil and garlic; saute until lightly brown. Raise the heat to high, toss in the shrimp, cabbage, tomato, tofu, and potato; stir-fry until the vegetables are tender but still crisp, 30 seconds to 1 minute. Add the noodles, salt, sugar, ketchup, and sriracha sauce; toss together to coat the noodles. Make a well in the middle of the wok; crack the eggs into the well and lightly scramble them, keeping them in the middle of the wok until they begin to set. Add the bean sprouts and quickly toss the mixture together until the eggs are cooked and the bean sprouts are wilted. Transfer to a platter and garnish with sliced chiles, celery leaves, Crisp Shallot Flakes, and a squeeze of lemon juice. Serve hot.

HAY MEE

Prawn Two-Noodle Soup
(*Chinese—Hokkien*)

In Singapore, *Hay Mee* is served as a one-dish lunch; it also makes a delicious light supper. *Mee* means noodles and *hay* means prawn (shrimp). The dish was originated by the Hokkien Chinese. Hokkien men married Malay women and established the large Nonya settlement in Penang, a port city in Malaysia. This recipe is in the Penang Nonya style, and contains such typical Nonya ingredients as chile paste, garlic, and shallots.

It is best to plan for this recipe in advance by freezing the shells and heads from all the shrimp you use for other dishes. That way you will always have enough shrimp shells on hand. Two pounds of shrimp will yield approximately 4 cups of loosely packed shells.

Serves 6

PRAWN SOUP
¼ pound large prawns (31 to 35 per pound)
1 tablespoon vegetable oil
4 cups loosely packed prawn shells and heads for stock
1½ pounds pork bones, preferably backbones
10 cups water

REMPAH
10 shallots (walnut-size) or 2 large onions, peeled
10 cloves garlic, peeled
⅓ cup dried shrimp, rinsed with water and drained
½ cup vegetable oil
⅓ cup Red Chile Paste (see page 39)

✿

1½ tablespoons salt
1½ tablespoons sugar
½ pound dried rice vermicelli (*bee hoon*)
½ pound Chinese thin egg noodles
3 cups fresh bean sprouts
3 cups cooked shredded chicken
6 hard-cooked eggs, peeled and cut into wedges
Chopped fresh Chinese chives
Crisp Shallot Flakes (page 166)

1. Shell and devein the prawns; poach or stir-fry them and set them aside. Reserve the shells.

2. Put the oil and shrimp shells and heads in a large saucepan. Brown the shells gently for 1 minute. Add the pork bones and water and bring it all to a boil. Skim off and discard the scum that rises to the surface. Reduce the heat and gently boil for 1½ hours.

3. While the stock cooks, prepare the *rempah*, as follows. Grind the shallots, garlic, and dried shrimp to a smooth paste in a blender or food processor. Add a tablespoon or more of water if needed to facilitate the blending. Heat the oil in a wok or saucepan and add the chile paste. Fry, stirring continuously, until the oil takes on a reddish hue, about 2 minutes. Add the ground mixture and fry over low heat, stirring frequently, until it combines completely with the oil. Continue frying until the *rempah* is fragrant and has a deep mahogany-red color and porridge-like consistency, about 8 minutes. It is ready when reddish oil seeps out.

4. Strain the stock into a saucepan; discard the shells and heads. Stir in the *rempah* and season with salt and sugar. Keep warm.

5. Cover the dried vermicelli with boiling water for 1 minute. Drain and set aside. Bring a large pot of water to a boil. Add the egg noodles. When the water reaches a second boil, drain the noodles in a colander. Rinse with cold water and drain.

6. To serve, divide both kinds of noodles among 6 soup bowls. Distribute the bean sprouts, shrimp, and chicken evenly on top of the noodles. Ladle hot stock over the noodles, arrange the hard-cooked eggs on top, and garnish with a generous sprinkling of chives and Crisp Shallot Flakes. Serve hot.

MEE SIAM

Rice Noodles in a Tangy Gravy with Seafood (*Nonya*)

Visitors to Singapore who eat this noodle dish go home with a vivid memory of its pungent flavors and a craving to match. The recipe may seem like a big production, but most of the components can be prepared in advance. The host of garnishes that are served with the noodles are optional; to the Singaporean palate, however, every one is a must. Serve *Mee Siam* as a luncheon dish and add a fresh fruit plate to complete the meal.

Serves 4

REMPAH
4 quarter-size slices fresh galangal, cut up (see Note, page 55)
5 candlenuts, soaked in water for 10 minutes, or skinless almonds
2 stalks fresh lemongrass, trimmed and sliced
10 shallots (walnut-size) or 2 large onions, peeled and halved
2 teaspoons *blachan* (dried shrimp paste)

¼ cup vegetable oil
2 tablespoons Red Chile Paste (see page 39)
1 tablespoon *tau cheo* (see Bean Sauces, page 28)

✿

2½ cups tamarind water (see page 41)
5 tablespoons sugar
2 teaspoons salt
1 pound dried rice vermicelli (*bee hoon*)
2 shallots
5 cloves garlic
¼ cup vegetable oil
1 tablespoon Red Chile Paste
1 pound fresh bean sprouts
1 tablespoon dried shrimp, soaked in water until soft and pliable (about 10 minutes)

GARNISHES
12 ounces large shrimp (31 to 35 per pound), poached
4 squares deep-fried tofu (see page 166), each cut into 3 strips
4 hard-cooked eggs, peeled and cut into wedges
1 cup chopped Chinese chives or green onions
2 limes, cut into quarters

1. To make the *rempah*, grind the galangal, candlenuts, lemongrass, shallots, and *blachan* to a smooth paste in a blender or food processor. Add a tablespoon or more of water if needed to facilitate the blending. Heat the oil in a wok or saucepan over medium heat. Add the chile paste and fry, stirring continuously, until the oil takes on a reddish hue, about 2 minutes. Add the ground mixture and the *tau cheo* and fry over low heat, stirring frequently, until the ingredients are completely combined. Continue frying until the *rempah* is fragrant and has a deep mahogany-red color and porridge-like consistency, about 8 minutes. It is ready when reddish oil seeps out. Add the tamarind water, 4½ tablespoons sugar, and 1 teaspoon salt, and simmer 5 minutes. Keep warm. This is the gravy.

2. Cover the dried vermicelli with boiling water for 1 minute. Drain and set aside. Grind the shallots and garlic to a paste in a mini-food processor or blender. Preheat a wok. Add the oil and red chile paste; fry over medium-high heat for 1 minute, stirring continuously to prevent the paste from burning. Add the garlic-shallot blend; fry for 30 seconds without browning. Add the noodles and the remaining sugar and salt and stir-fry until the noodles are stained with red. Toss in the bean sprouts and the rehydrated shrimp; stir-fry until the bean sprouts begin to wilt, about 1 minute.

3. To serve, divide the noodles among 4 soup bowls. Pour the hot gravy over the noodles and top each bowl with some poached shrimp, fried tofu, hard-cooked eggs, chives, and lime wedges for squeezing. Serve hot.

MEE KARABU

Dry-Style Noodles with Lemon and Toasted Coconut
(*Nonya*)

Singaporean hawker cooks have responded to the popularity of Thai-style noodles by creating their own interpretations and variations, many of which barely resemble the original. This version has rice vermicelli noodles tossed in a tangy, sweet-sour, and savory sauce that resembles a salad dressing, making this dish much like a noodle salad.

Serves 2

¼ pound firm fresh bean curd (tofu)
Vegetable oil for deep-frying
¼ pound dried rice vermicelli (*bee hoon*), soaked in water until soft (about 15 minutes) and drained
¼ cup dried shrimp, soaked in water until soft (about 15 minutes) and drained
⅓ cup grated unsweetened coconut
1 teaspoon *Sambal Blachan* (page 161)
4 shallots, sliced
Juice of ½ lemon
1 teaspoon sugar
⅛ teaspoon salt
1 stalk Chinese celery or regular celery, chopped
Crisp Shallot Flakes (page 166)

1. Pat the bean curd dry thoroughly. Cut it in half horizontally, then into ¼-inch cubes. Fill a wok or saucepan no more than half full with oil. Heat the oil to 365°F, add the bean curd, and deep-fry until golden brown, about 3 to 4 minutes; set aside.

2. While the noodles and shrimp are soaking, toast the grated coconut in an ungreased skillet until light golden brown. Drain the noodles and shrimp separately.

3. Grind the dried shrimp as finely as possible in a blender or mini-food processor. Transfer it to a bowl and mix in the *sambal blachan,* shallots, lemon juice, sugar, and salt. This is the dressing.

4. Dip the drained noodles in a pan of boiling water to heat them through. Drain. Toss the noodles thoroughly with the dressing, toasted coconut, and fried bean curd. Top with chopped celery and Crisp Shallot Flakes. Serve at room temperature.

CHOW KWAY TEO

Stir-Fried Rice Noodles with Shrimp and Chinese Sausage
(*Chinese—Teochew*)

This easy-to-prepare dish is a popular Singaporean hawker food. A delicious mixture of seafood, sausage, bean sprouts, and scrambled egg are stir-fried together with *kway teo*, the flat ribbon-style fresh rice noodles popular among the southern Chinese. The dish reflects the cooking style of Teochew, a region in southern China. If fresh rice noodles are not available, dried ones will work.

Serves 2; serves 4 as a snack or with other dishes

1½ tablespoons vegetable oil
½ tablespoon chopped garlic
4 ounces large shrimp (31 to 35 per pound), shelled, deveined, and cut in half lengthwise
1 Chinese sausage, thinly sliced diagonally
1 ounce fried fish cake, thinly sliced (see Note, page 81)
¾ pound fresh flat ribbon-shaped rice noodles
1 tablespoon Thai fish sauce
2 tablespoons Thai sweet soy sauce (Kwong Hong Seng brand) or 2 tablespoons dark soy sauce mixed with ½ tablespoon sugar
1 tablespoon sriracha sauce
1 egg
1 large handful bean sprouts
1 green onion, chopped

Preheat a wok over medium-high heat. When hot, add the oil and garlic; saute until lightly brown. Increase the heat to high. Toss in the shrimp, sausage, and fish cake and stir-fry until the shrimp turn bright orange. Add the noodles, fish sauce, sweet soy sauce, and sriracha sauce; toss together to coat the noodles. Make a well in the middle of the wok; crack the egg into it. Lightly scramble the egg, being careful not to mix it with the other foods. When the egg begins to set, in 5 to 10 seconds, add the bean sprouts and toss the mixture together until the sprouts begin to wilt and the egg is fully cooked and speckles the mixture. Transfer to a serving plate and garnish with green onions. Serve hot.

HOKKIEN BEE HOON

Rice Noodles Stir-Fried with Seafood
(*Chinese—Hokkien*)

This Straits Cafe version of a traditional noodle dish uses both fresh and dried rice noodles. The fresh *laksa* noodles are the size and shape of spaghetti, with a smooth and slippery texture. The dried rice noodles have a meatier texture. Both readily absorb flavors. Traditionally, fresh unsmoked bacon is boiled and cut into small pieces and fried with the noodles for added flavor.

The wok chefs at the Cafe stir-fry these noodles over an awesome 30,000-BTU stove; they execute the dish in less than a minute. The recipe has been slightly altered to fit the capabilities of a domestic gas or electric stove.

Serves 2 to 4

¼ pound *bee hoon* (dried rice stick noodles)
2 ounces fresh *laksa* noodles
3 tablespoons oil (approximately)
1 teaspoon chopped garlic
¼ pound large shrimp (31 to 35 per pound), shelled, deveined, and split in half lengthwise
½ cup fried fish cakes, sliced ¼ inch thick (see Note)
¼ pound cleaned squid with tentacles, bodies cut into ½-inch rings
1 red serrano or jalapeño chile, sliced
2 teaspoons Thai fish sauce
1 large handful fresh bean sprouts
1 egg
1 green onion, chopped
½ cup chicken stock
¼ teaspoon salt (optional)
Fresh coriander leaves, for garnish
Lemon wedges, for garnish

1. In separate bowls, scald the dried rice stick noodles and laksa noodles in boiling water for 1 minute. Drain separately and set aside.

2. Heat a wok over medium heat. When the wok is hot add 2 tablespoons of oil and the garlic; saute until golden brown. Toss in the shrimp, fish cakes, squid, and chile; stir-fry until the shrimp begin to turn bright orange and the squid turns opaque, about 30 seconds. Sprinkle with fish sauce and toss together. (If you are concerned about overcooking the seafood, remove the mixture from the wok to a plate and add it back to the wok at the end.)

3. Add a tablespoon of oil, or more if the wok seems dry. Add all the noodles. Toss quickly for a minute, then push the ingredients up the wok sides and add the bean sprouts into the center; toss and stir-fry together until the sprouts begin to wilt. Again push the food up the wok sides

and break the egg into the middle. Lightly scramble it with the tip of the spatula in the center of the wok. Let it set a moment, then toss it together with the other ingredients until the egg is cooked and speckles the noodles. Add the green onion and chicken stock, stir for a second, and cover the wok for 1 minute or until the noodles are moistened with stock. If you removed the seafood mixture, return it to the wok now. Quickly toss everything together. Season with salt, if needed. Transfer the mixture to a platter; garnish with fresh coriander and lemon wedges.

NOTE: Fried fish cakes are available in the refrigerated section of Asian markets. They are called Chiu Chow fish cakes.

LONTONG
Rice Cooked in Banana Leaves
(*Indonesian/Malay*)

Lontong is rice formed into a compact block so that it can be sliced or picked up and eaten with the fingers, and so it is easily transportable. Traditionally *lontong* was cooked in a hollow bamboo tube or tightly wrapped in banana leaves. Chris cooks it in a heavy-duty sealed plastic bag. Serve *Lontong* rice packets with *Sayur Lodeh* (Vegetables in Spicy Coconut Curry, page 96) or cut into cubes for *Soto Ayam* (Spicy Chicken Soup, page 64).

Makes 20 ½-inch slices

1½ cups raw long-grain rice

Wash the rice with cold water until the water runs clear. Drain. Pour the rice into the bottom of a gallon-size self-sealing plastic bag. Let it spread evenly across the bottom of the bag. Fold over the top, leaving enough space for the rice to triple in volume when cooked. Seal the top edge with staples or toothpicks. Put the bag into another bag and seal the top. With the sharp tip of a skewer, pierce both bags in several spots to let out excess air. Choose a pot large enough to accommodate the length of the bag. Put in the bag and add enough cold water to completely cover it. Bring the water to a boil and cook the rice at a gentle boil for 1½ hours. Add more boiling water if needed. Remove the bag and allow the rice to cool in it. When the rice is cool, refrigerate it until cold, at least 4 hours. Remove it from the bag and cut it into ½-inch slices or cubes.

NASI GORENG

Malaysian-Style Fried Rice
(*Malay*)

If you have leftover rice, do as every cook in Asia does and make fried rice. Although fried rice originated in China, every Asian country has its own version. *Nasi Goreng,* a blend of Indonesian and Malay cooking styles, is filled with shrimp, peas, carrots, cabbage, and eggs. This Straits Cafe version uses two kinds of rice—plain steamed long-grain rice and coconut-simmered rice. If you do not have leftovers of both kinds of rice, use all plain steamed rice or all coconut rice. Serve the dish, as they do in Singapore, for breakfast, lunch, or as a snack, topped with a crisp fried egg, sunny side up.

Serves 4 to 6

1½ cups cooked long-grain rice, cold
1½ cups coconut-simmered rice (*Nasi Lemak,* page 83), cold
2 tablespoons oil from Red Chile Paste (page 39) or vegetable oil
1 tablespoon chopped garlic
1 cup cabbage in ¾-inch cubes
¼ pound medium shrimp (41 to 50 per pound), shelled, deveined, and cut crosswise into thirds
1 large egg
¼ cup cooked carrots in ¼-inch dice
¼ cup blanched peas
1 tablespoon sriracha sauce or Red Chile Paste (see page 39)
1 tablespoon Thai fish sauce
1 teaspoon salt, or to taste
Pinch of sugar
Crisp Shallot Flakes (page 166)

1. Put the rice in a plastic bag and gently press the lumps to separate the grains; set aside.

2. Preheat a wok over medium heat. When hot, add the oil and garlic; saute until lightly brown. Toss in the cabbage and stir-fry for 1 minute or until it begins to wilt. Add the shrimp and stir-fry until they turn bright orange, about 30 seconds. Increase the heat to high, push the ingredients up the sides of the wok, and crack the egg into the middle. Lightly scramble it in the middle of the wok until it begins to set. Add the rice, carrots, peas, sriracha sauce or chile paste, fish sauce, salt, and sugar. Stir-fry until all the rice is evenly coated with the sauce. Garnish with Crisp Shallot Flakes. Serve hot.

NASI LEMAK
Fragrant Rice Simmered in Coconut Milk
(*Malay*)

Nasi Lemak is basically long-grain rice simmered in coconut milk and seasoned with pandan leaf. Delicious garnishes which accompany the rice include *ikan bilis* (crisp-fried anchovies) mixed with fried peanuts, cucumber, and slices of hard boiled egg. This dish, topped with *Sambal Udang* (Prawns Sauteed in Chile-Shallot Sambal) is eaten as breakfast in Malaysia and Singapore.

Serves 6

2 cups long-grain rice
¾ cup coconut milk (shake can well before measuring)
1¼ cups water, or enough to cover rice by 1 inch
½ teaspoon salt, plus more to taste
2 fresh or frozen pandan leaves (*daun pandan*—optional)
¼ cup *ikan bilis* (crisp fried anchovies)
1 cup deep-fried peanuts
Pinch of sugar
1 cucumber, sliced
***Sambal Udang* (page 114)**
Slices of hard-cooked egg

1. Put the rice in a large bowl and rinse it with cold water until the water looks clear; drain thoroughly. Combine the rice, coconut milk, water, and ½ teaspoon of salt in a saucepan. Boil over high heat until there is no water left on the surface of the rice. If using pandan leaves, tie each into a knot and place them on top of the rice. Cover the pot, reduce the heat, and simmer until steam no longer seeps through the cover, about 10 minutes. Turn off the heat and allow the rice to finish cooking for another 10 minutes. Do not remove the cover.

2. Combine the *ikan bilis* and peanuts; season to taste with salt and sugar.

3. Fluff the rice with a wet wooden spoon; discard the pandan leaves. For each serving, put 1 cup of rice on a banana leaf or plate. Scatter a small portion of the *ikan bilis* mixture, cucumber slices, *sambal udang,* and hard-cooked egg on top. Serve hot or at room temperature.

NASI KUNYIT
Turmeric Rice with Coconut Milk
(*Nonya*)

Nasi Kunyit is made with sweet glutinous rice, a short-grain variety also known as sticky rice. Flavored with coconut milk, colored with turmeric, and scented with pandan leaves, the rice sparkles with a golden hue and has a subtle exotic fragrance. *Nasi Kunyit* is traditionally steamed; however, if you prefer, you may boil it as you normally do rice. Serve it with "wet"-style curries.

Makes 6 to 7 cups

2 pounds glutinous rice (4½ cups raw rice)
3 tablespoons turmeric powder
2 pandan leaves (*daun pandan*)
1 teaspoon white peppercorns
1 cup thick unsweetened coconut milk
1 teaspoon salt

1. Wash the rice with cold water until the water runs clear. Cover the rice with cold water and soak for at least a few hours or overnight. Drain. Mix the turmeric with the rice; let it sit for 1 hour. Rinse with cold water and drain. If the turmeric is not rinsed out, the rice will be pasty.

2. Line a steaming tray with a tea towel (or cut a piece of banana leaf to line the tray). Spread the rice on top in a layer no thicker than 2 inches, leaving a 3-inch circle in the center empty. If using banana leaf, prick several holes in the center. Steam over boiling water for 40 minutes. Check the water frequently and replenish with boiling water when needed. During the last 5 minutes, place the pandan leaves and white peppercorns on top of the rice. When the rice is cooked, transfer it to a bowl. Discard the pandan leaves and stir in the coconut milk and salt.

INDIAN FRY BREAD

(*Indian*)

This Indian fried bread is like a puffy herb-seasoned donut. It is mainly used to sop up the extra sauce and juices of curry dishes. It is a wonderful accompaniment to the Beef Tandoori on page 148.

Makes 12

1 cup milk
2 cups all-purpose flour, plus more for kneading
2 teaspoons baking powder
½ teaspoon salt
1 teaspoon turmeric powder
1 tablespoon ground coriander
4 tablespoons chopped green onions
Vegetable oil for deep-frying

1. Heat the milk in a saucepan. Thoroughly combine the flour, baking powder, salt, turmeric, and coriander in a mixing bowl. Mix in the green onions. Pour in ¾ cup of the warm milk in a steady stream and mix with a large wooden spoon or your fingers into a rough mass. Add more milk until the dough feels soft and spongy and a bit sticky. If the dough still feels dry, add a tablespoon or more additional milk until you have a smooth dough. It may seem too moist and unmanageable, but continue to knead and dust with flour until it is smooth and elastic. Cover and set aside to rest for 1 hour. (The dough may be made ahead to this point, covered, and refrigerated. Thirty minutes before you are ready to roll it out, remove it from the refrigerator.)

2. Pinch off a 1-inch piece of dough (1/12 of the whole). Lightly dust the palms of your hands and knead the dough into a smooth ball. Flatten it in your palm into a 4-inch round that is no more than ¼ inch thick. Repeat with the remaining dough and keep the rounds covered until you are ready to fry.

3. Preheat a wok, saucepan, or deep-fryer. Add 2 to 3 inches of oil and heat it to 365°F. Add a few rounds of dough. Pat them down with a slotted spoon so that they will fry evenly. The bread should puff up within 30 seconds. When a round stops sizzling and the bottom is golden brown, gently turn it over and brown the other side, about 30 seconds longer. Remove with a slotted spoon and drain on paper towels. Repeat with the remaining rounds. If you want to serve the bread puffed up, serve immediately. The deflated breads are just as good and can be reheated in a preheated 300°F oven for 10 minutes.

ROTI PRATA
Indian Griddled Bread
(*Indian*)

The idea of griddled bread comes from India. *Roti Prata* was most likely brought to Singapore by early Indian traders. Instead of using *atta* or whole wheat flour, local cooks used the plain flour available to them to make a multi-layer flaky pastry bread.

The *prata* man, as he is called by the locals, is usually Indian. He skillfully flips the dough into the air (almost like pizza dough) stretching it until it is paper-thin, then folds it into several layers and fries it on a hot oiled griddle. The *roti prata* comes out with a wonderful chewy and flaky texture. In Singapore, it is served for breakfast; diners tear pieces off and dip them in a mild chicken curry (*Patong Ayam*, page 142). *Roti Prata* served as a side dish with a garden salad makes a nice light lunch. Note that the dough must rest at least 5 hours before griddling, so it is best to start the night before.

Makes 8

3½ cups flour, plus more for rolling
1 teaspoon salt
½ cup plus 5 tablespoons melted ghee or margarine
1¼ cups warm milk
3 to 6 tablespoons vegetable oil

1. Sift the flour and salt into a large bowl. Add 5 tablespoons of ghee and stir until the mixture looks crumbly. Slowly pour in the milk and mix with your hands. The dough will feel soft, spongy, and almost too sticky. Knead the dough without adding extra flour until it pulls away from the bowl and forms a smooth ball. Continue kneading until the dough feels just slightly sticky, about 10 minutes.

2. Cut the dough into 8 pieces. Roll each piece into a ball, flatten it slightly, and rub it with ghee. Place the flattened balls on a tray. Cover the tray with a damp cloth and let the dough rest for at least 5 hours. (If you make the dough the night before, cover the tray with plastic wrap and refrigerate overnight.)

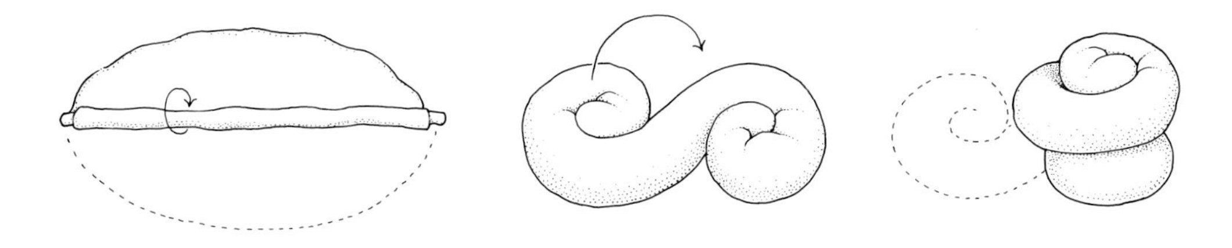

1. Roll the dough into a long rope. 2. Coil the ends. 3. Fold one coil on top of the other.

3. Lightly oil a rolling pin and work surface with ghee. Roll out one ball, stretching the dough into a paper-thin circle, about 9 inches in diameter. Lightly brush the dough with ghee and lightly sprinkle it with flour. Starting at the bottom edge, roll up the circle jelly-roll style until you have a long rope. Gently pull the ends to stretch it an inch longer. Take one end and roll it clockwise into a coil until it reaches the center of the rope. Roll the opposite end clockwise until the two coils meet in the middle. Fold one coil over on top of the other. Press the two coils gently together into one thick round. Wrap it with plastic wrap and set it aside for 1 hour. Repeat with the remaining balls.

4. On a lightly floured surface, roll out one round into a 6- to 7-inch circle. (It is best to roll out only the *rotis* you will be serving immediately; keep the rest individually wrapped in plastic.) Heat a griddle or skillet over medium heat; grease it with about 1 teaspoon each of vegetable oil and ghee. Fry the *roti* gently for about 2 minutes or until the bottom is nicely browned. Turn it over, add a teaspoon more oil or ghee, and fry a minute longer. When the bottom is golden brown and speckled and the *roti* is puffy, remove it and drain it on a paper towel. Fry as many *rotis* as you are going to serve, one at a time. Serve hot with *Patong Ayam.* To eat, tear the *roti* into pieces and dip it into the chicken curry.

NOTE: *To mix the dough in a food processor:* put the flour and salt into the workbowl and pulse to mix. Dribble the melted ghee over the flour and pulse until the mixture is crumbly, about 10 seconds. While the machine is running, pour 1 cup plus 2 tablespoons of the warm milk down the feed tube; process until a ball of dough forms and pulls away from the sides of the workbowl. Remove the dough and knead it on a flat surface for 5 to 10 minutes or until it feels spongy, elastic, and just a bit sticky to the touch. Try to refrain from dusting with flour; if needed, use only enough to keep the dough from sticking to your hands and the work surface. Continue with step 2.

MURTABAK
Spicy Meat-Stuffed Griddled Bread
(*Indian*)

Singapore is known for its fabulous Indian cooking. Indian coffee shops and street hawkers serve an unbelievable assortment of griddled breads, known as *roti* or *chapati* breads, that are light, flaky, and slightly chewy. *Murtabak,* a very popular snack, is spicy ground meat encased in *roti* bread and browned on a griddle until crisp. Murtabak served with a salad makes a great luncheon entree.

Makes 8

1 recipe *Roti Prata* (page 86)

REMPAH
4 1-inch chunks fresh ginger, peeled and sliced
10 shallots (walnut size) or 2 large onions, peeled and sliced
6 cloves garlic, peeled and sliced
1/3 cup vegetable oil
1/3 cup Red Chile Paste (see page 39)
2 1/2 tablespoons fresh or frozen curry leaves

✿

2 1/2 tablespoons Indian-style curry powder
1 medium onion, chopped
1 pound ground beef
1 teaspoon salt
2 tablespoons sugar
2 stalks Chinese celery or regular celery, chopped (about 1/3 cup)
2 eggs
Ghee or vegetable oil for frying

1. Prepare the *Roti Prata* recipe through step 3. Set aside.

2. To prepare the *rempah,* grind the ginger, shallots, and garlic to a smooth paste in a blender or food processor. Add a tablespoon or more of water if needed to facilitate the blending. Heat the oil in a wok or saucepan. When hot, carefully add the Red Chile Paste and curry leaves; fry over medium heat for 2 minutes, stirring continuously, until the oil takes on a reddish hue. Add the ground mixture and fry, stirring frequently, until the *rempah* is fragrant and has a deep mahogany-red color and porridge-like consistency, about 8 minutes. It is ready when reddish oil seeps out.

3. Mix in the curry powder and onion. Lightly saute until the onion is limp. Raise the heat and add the beef, salt, and sugar. Stir-fry, breaking up the lumps, until the meat is cooked but tender, about 5 minutes; do not brown. Add the celery and stir-fry for a few seconds. The mixture should be crumbly. Transfer it to a bowl and set aside to cool. When cool, beat in the eggs.

4. Place one bread round on a flat surface. With your fingertips spread it into an 8-inch circle. Put 3 heaping tablespoons of the meat mixture in the center of the circle, leaving 2 inches of dough all around. Fold two opposite sides of dough into the center, overlapping them by 1/2 inch. Fold over the remaining two sides to enclose the package. Press down gently to form a square.

5. Lightly oil a griddle or frying pan. Put a *murtabak* fold side down on the griddle and fry over low heat until golden brown, about 5 minutes on each side. Repeat with the remaining dough and filling. Serve hot.

NOTE: *Murtabak* may be refrigerated; reheat in a 425°F oven for 10 minutes or microwave at high power for 1 minute. They can also be frozen; thaw for 1 hour before reheating.

Roti Prata (page 86)

VEGETABLES

Sweet and Sour Peppers and Eggplant (page 97)

KANGKONG SAMBAL

Spicy Chinese Water Spinach with Prawns
(*Nonya/Malay*)

Kangkong is no longer a stranger in America. It is seasonal (winter to early fall) and can be found in Asian markets. Technically called water convolvulus, *kangkong* (*ong choy* in Cantonese) tastes like a cross between spinach and watercress and can be used like either of them. The stem is long, often more than a foot, with spear-shaped leaves at the very end. Use the leaves and no more than an inch or two of the connecting stem. In this dish *kangkong* is stir-fried in a shallot-garlic-chile *rempah* with the subtle sweet-fruity flavor of tamarind. In an Asian meal it would be served as one of many entrees, but you can also serve it as a vegetable with pan-fried pork chops or broiled lamb chops.

Serves 4 to 6 with other dishes

1 pound *kangkong*, or fresh spinach or watercress

REMPAH
4 fresh red jalapeño chiles, seeded
5 shallots (walnut-size) or 1 large onion, peeled and sliced
6 cloves garlic, peeled and sliced
1 slice *blachan* (dried shrimp paste), 1 inch square by ¼ inch thick
¼ cup vegetable oil
¼ pound large shrimp (31 to 35 per pound), shelled and deveined
¼ cup tamarind water (see page 41)
¼ teaspoon sugar
½ teaspoon salt

1. Trim all but 1 inch of the stems from the *kangkong*; discard. Rinse the leaves in a basin of cold water until thoroughly free of sand and grit. Pat dry thoroughly or spin in a lettuce spinner.

2. To make the *rempah*, grind the chiles, shallots, garlic, and *blachan* to a smooth paste in a blender or mini-food processor. Add a tablespoon or more of water if needed to facilitate the blending. Heat the oil in a wok or saucepan over medium-high heat. Add the ground mixture, lower the heat, and fry over low heat, stirring frequently, until the *rempah* has the consistency of dry porridge and is fragrant, about 5 minutes.

3. Raise the heat to medium-high and add the shrimp. Stir-fry for 15 seconds, leaving the shrimp slightly undercooked. Raise the heat to high and toss in the *kangkong* and tamarind water. Stir-fry quickly until all the liquid has evaporated. You may need to push the *kangkong* up the sides of the wok to allow the juices on the bottom to reduce. When the leaves are wilted and the pan is dry, season with sugar and salt. Transfer the *kangkong* to a platter and serve hot.

LONG BEAN SAMBAL
(*Nonya/Malay*)

Chinese long green beans come in two varieties. One is dark green and pencil-thin, the other light green and slightly fatter. The former has a finer taste and crispier texture and is a better choice for this recipe. You can find them in Chinese markets during most of the year. Regular supermarket string beans or French green beans will also give you delicious results.

Serves 4 with other dishes

1½ tablespoons dried shrimp

REMPAH
5 fresh red jalapeño chiles, seeded
8 shallots (walnut-size) or 2 medium onions, peeled and sliced
5 cloves garlic, peeled and sliced
1 slice *blachan* (dried shrimp paste), 1 inch square by ¼ inch thick
¼ cup vegetable oil

✿

8 ounces long green beans, trimmed and cut into 1-inch lengths
⅓ cup water
1 teaspoon sugar
½ teaspoon salt

1. Cover the dried shrimp with water for 10 minutes. Drain. Mince fine in a blender or mini-food processor and set aside.

2. To make the *rempah*, grind the chiles, shallots, garlic, and *blachan* to a smooth paste in a blender or food processor. Add a tablespoon or more of water if needed to facilitate the blending. Heat the oil in a wok or saucepan over medium heat. Add the ground mixture and fry, stirring frequently, until it is completely combined with the oil, about 3 to 5 minutes. When the *rempah* is fragrant and has the consistency of dry porridge and oil seeps out, it is cooked. Add the minced shrimp; cook over medium-high heat until the mixture is crumbly, a minute or 2. Toss in the green beans; stir-fry for 1 minute. Add the water and season with sugar and salt. Stir-fry quickly until the sauce reduces and glazes the beans.

NONYA CHAP CHYE

A Vegetarian Medley
(*Nonya*)

There are many versions of *Chap Chye*. Some are very simple. Others, like this one served at the Straits Cafe, are a wonderful medley of fresh and dried vegetables. *Chap Chye* makes a complete vegetarian-style meal. To make it totally vegetarian, use fermented soybean sauce (*tau cheo*) in place of oyster sauce as the seasoning condiment.

Serves 4 to 6 as a side dish

⅓ cup dried lily buds (golden needles)
4 to 6 Chinese dried black mushrooms
1½ ounces mung bean thread noodles
1 carrot
6 dried bean curd sheets (optional)
Vegetable oil
1 tablespoon chopped garlic
1 cup green cabbage cut in 1-inch cubes
1 cup purple cabbage cut in 1-inch cubes
⅓ cup rice wine
⅓ cup oyster sauce
1 teaspoon sugar
½ teaspoon salt

1. In separate bowls, cover the lily buds, black mushrooms, and bean thread noodles with water until they are soft and pliable, about 20 minutes.

2. Drain the lily buds and snap off the hard ends; set aside. Remove the mushrooms and gently squeeze out the excess water. Cut off and discard the stems; cut the caps into slices about ⅓ inch wide. Set aside. Drain the noodles. If you prefer them shorter, cut them into thirds or manageable lengths with kitchen shears. Set aside. Cut the carrot diagonally into ⅛-inch slices; blanch the slices and set them aside.

3. With kitchen shears cut the dried bean curd sheets into quarters. Preheat a wok. Add 1 inch of oil and heat it to 365°F. Add the pieces of dried bean curd and deep-fry until light golden brown, about 30 seconds. Drain on paper towels.

4. Spoon out all the oil except 2 tablespoons. Stir-fry the garlic over medium heat until light golden brown. Increase the heat to high and add the lily buds, mushrooms, carrots, and cabbage; stir-fry for 1 minute. Toss in the bean curd sheets, noodles, rice wine, oyster sauce, sugar, and salt; toss together for 1 minute longer. If the mixture seems dry, add some water to moisten the vegetables. When the vegetables are tender but still crisp transfer them to a platter and serve hot.

SAYUR LODEH

Vegetables in Spicy Coconut Curry
(*Indonesian/Malay*)

In Western terms, this vegetable dish is somewhere between a stew and a soup. It originated in Indonesia, where it is very popular among the village and country people. The flavor is lively and exciting, yet mellow and savory. Other vegetables with similar textures and colors may be substituted. Do not hesitate to make the full recipe; it is a large batch, but it tastes better with time.

Serves 6 to 8

REMPAH
1 quarter-size slice fresh galangal, cut up (see Note, page 55)
2 stalks fresh lemongrass, trimmed and sliced
4 shallots (walnut-size) or 1 onion, peeled and sliced
4 cloves garlic, peeled and sliced
½ teaspoon *blachan* (dried shrimp paste)
¼ cup dried shrimp, rinsed and drained
¼ cup vegetable oil
2 tablespoons Red Chile Paste (see page 39)

✿

1 can (13½ ounces) unsweetened coconut milk, plus 1 can water
1 carrot, sliced diagonally
1 Chinese eggplant, cut into quarters lengthwise then into 2-inch lengths
¼ head cabbage, in 1½-inch cubes
1 potato-size chunk jicama, cut into julienne sticks ¼ inch thick by 2 inches long
1 cup Chinese long beans or green beans, cut in 2-inch lengths
1 square fried tempeh, cut into 1-inch pieces or 6 squares deep-fried bean curd (*dou fu pok*)
1 teaspoon sugar
¾ teaspoon salt

1. To make the *rempah*, grind the galangal, lemongrass, shallots, garlic, *blachan*, and dried shrimp to a smooth paste in a blender or food processor. Add a tablespoon or more of water if needed to facilitate the blending. Heat the oil in a wok or saucepan. Add the chile paste and fry, stirring continuously, until the oil takes on a reddish hue, about 2 minutes. Add the ground mixture. Fry over low heat, stirring frequently, until the *rempah* is very fragrant and has a rich mahogany-red color and porridge-like consistency, about 8 minutes. It is ready when reddish oil seeps out.

2. Add the coconut milk and water and bring to a boil, stirring frequently to prevent the coconut cream from curdling. Reduce the heat to medium and add the carrot, eggplant, cabbage, jicama, long beans, and tempeh. Simmer until the vegetables are cooked, about 15 minutes. Season with sugar and salt. Serve hot with or over rice.

SWEET AND SOUR PEPPERS AND EGGPLANT
(Nonya)

The rich, well-balanced sweet and sour glaze on this vegetable dish makes it especially popular at the Straits Cafe. The eggplant is deep-fried, which is, of course, easy with a restaurant's built-in deep-fryer. It's fine if you prefer to saute or bake the eggplant; both methods work well.

Serves 2 to 4 with other dishes

2 large Chinese eggplants (see Note)
Vegetable oil
1 teaspoon chopped garlic
½ onion, sliced
½ red bell pepper, sliced
½ green bell pepper, sliced
⅓ cup chicken stock
¼ cup oyster sauce
⅓ cup white vinegar
3 tablespoons sugar
1 tablespoon rice wine
1 teaspoon sesame oil
1 teaspoon cornstarch dissolved in 1 tablespoon water
1 teaspoon toasted sesame seeds

1. Cut the eggplants in half lengthwise then crosswise into thirds. Preheat a wok, pour in 2 inches of oil, and heat it to 365°F. Carefully lower the eggplant into the oil and deep-fry until golden brown, about 4 to 5 minutes. Remove and drain. Ladle out all but 1 tablespoon of oil.

2. Add the garlic, onion and red and green peppers to the wok. Stir-fry over high heat until tender but still crisp. Add the chicken stock, oyster sauce, vinegar, sugar, rice wine, and sesame oil; bring to a boil. Add the cornstarch and stir together until the sauce turns into a glaze. Return the eggplant to the wok. Toss to reheat and coat with the sauce. Top with the toasted sesame seeds.

NOTE: The elongated Asian eggplant is sweeter and more tender than Western eggplant, and it is nearly seedless. The Chinese variety is long and lavender while Japanese eggplant (which may be substituted) is smaller and a deep, almost black purple. Unlike the Western globe-shaped eggplant, Asian eggplants do not need to be peeled, unless for aesthetic reasons. If Asian eggplant is not available, use 1 peeled Western eggplant.

LADY FINGERS SAMBAL

(*Nonya/Malay*)

In the West, okra is not usually thought of as an Asian vegetable, as it came into American cooking from Africa. According to *A World of Vegetable Cookery* by Alex D. Hawkes, however, okra originated in the Asiatic tropics. With that in mind, it seems natural that Asians have an affinity for okra. In this dish fresh okra is stir-fried with tamarind until tender but still crisp.

[I never disliked okra, I just didn't like it—until Chris served it to me at the Straits Cafe with a slightly sweet, sour, garlicky, and snappy "dry" glaze-like sauce. Overnight, I became a convert. J.J.]

Serves 4 to 6 with other dishes

1½ tablespoons dried shrimp
½-inch cube tamarind pulp
¾ cup boiling water
6 ounces fresh okra

REMPAH
5 fresh red jalapeño chiles, seeded
8 shallots (walnut-size) or 2 medium onions, peeled and sliced
5 cloves garlic, peeled and sliced
1 slice *blachan* (dried shrimp paste), about 1 inch square by ¼ inch thick
¼ cup vegetable oil

✿

1 teaspoon sugar
½ teaspoon salt

1. Cover the dried shrimp with water; soak for 10 minutes.

2. Put the tamarind pulp in a bowl with the boiling water; break up the pulp with a fork to help dissolve it. Let it sit for 10 minutes, then pour the liquid through a fine mesh strainer into a bowl; use the back of a spoon to force the pulp through and press out the liquid. Scrape the pulp clinging to the underside of the strainer into the bowl. Discard the seeds and fibers. Set the tamarind water aside.

3. While the tamarind soaks, snap off and discard the okra stems. Cut each okra diagonally into 3 or 4 pieces; set aside. Drain the shrimp and pat them dry. Mince them finely in a blender or mini-food processor; set aside.

4. To make the *rempah*, grind the chiles, shallots, garlic, and *blachan* to a smooth paste in a blender or food processor. Add a tablespoon or more of water if needed to facilitate the blending. Heat the oil in a wok or saucepan over medium heat. Add the ground mixture and fry over low heat, stirring frequently, until the *rempah* is fragrant and has the consistency of porridge, about 5 minutes. Increase the heat to high and add the minced shrimp; cook until thick and crumbly, 1 to 2 minutes. Toss in the okra and stir-fry for 1 minute. Add the tamarind liquid, season with sugar and salt, and stir-fry quickly until the sauce reduces and clings to the okra.

STUFFED BEAN CURD, EGGPLANT, BITTER MELON, AND PEPPERS

(*Chinese—Hakka*)

Vegetables stuffed with a delicate fish mousse is a Hakka Chinese specialty. Chef Jenny Fong at the Straits Cafe stuffs a variety of vegetables for this dish, but you do not need to include all of them. For a wonderful appetizer or first course, stuff just one vegetable and serve it as part of a Western menu.

Serves 8

2 squares fresh firm tofu (bean curd)
1 Chinese eggplant
1 bitter melon
1 green bell pepper
4 red jalapeño chiles
1 pound fresh fish puree (see Note)
¼ teaspoon white pepper
3 green onions, green tops only, thinly sliced
Vegetable oil for deep-frying

GARLIC OYSTER SAUCE
2 tablespoons vegetable oil
½ tablespoon minced garlic
2½ cups water
⅓ cup oyster sauce
3 tablespoons cornstarch dissolved in ¼ cup water
½ tablespoon Asian sesame oil

✿

Chopped green onions, for garnish

1. Pat the tofu dry. Cut each square diagonally in half. Make a cut into the long edge of each half, then with a teaspoon dig into the center and scoop out a pocket. Be sure to leave ¼-inch-thick sides all around. Set aside.

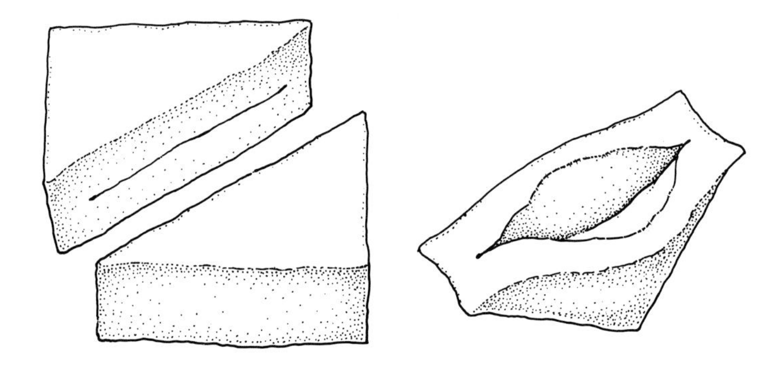

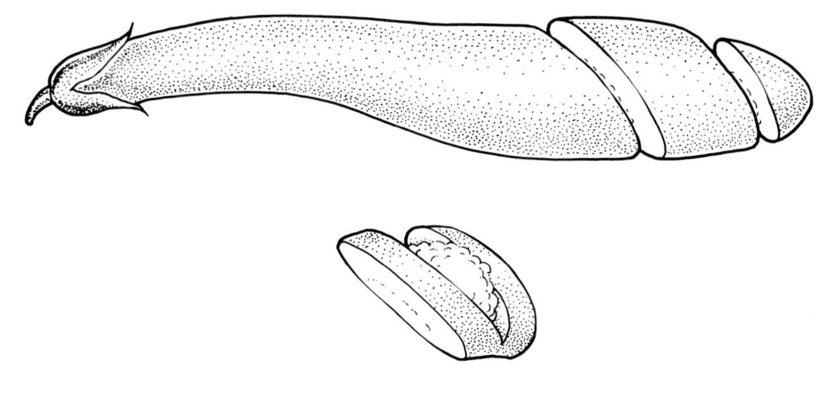

2. Cut the eggplant diagonally into ¾-inch-thick slices. Make a cut through the middle leaving one end intact to make an eggplant "fan" sandwich. Set aside.

3. Cut the bitter melon diagonally into ½-inch-thick slices. Scrape out and discard the pulp and seeds. Set aside.

4. Cut off the top of the bell pepper and scrape out the seeds. Cut the pepper vertically into quarters, then cut each quarter crosswise into thirds. Set aside.

5. Slice off a lengthwise strip from 3 of the jalapeño chiles. Remove and discard the stem and seeds. Set aside. Finely chop the remaining chile.

6. To make the mousse filling, thoroughly mix the fish puree, chopped chile, white pepper, and sliced green onions. Use the filling to stuff the tofu pockets. Spread it in the middle of the eggplant "sandwiches." Fill the bitter melon slices, pepper sections, and chiles. Neatly smooth the fish mousse so that it lays flat against the vegetables. Dip your hands into water or oil and roll the remaining mousse into 1-inch balls.

7. Fill a wok or saucepan no more than half full of oil; heat the oil to 365°F. Deep-fry the fish balls until golden brown, about 2 minutes. Deep-fry the stuffed vegetables and tofu in batches for 2 to 3 minutes or until they turn golden brown. As they are done, remove and drain them on paper towels. Keep them warm in the oven until all are done.

8. To make the sauce, heat 2 tablespoons of oil in a wok or large skillet over medium heat. Add the garlic and saute until light golden brown. Stir in the water and oyster sauce. Place the fried vegetables in the pan in one layer; simmer for 3 minutes. With a slotted spoon remove the vegetables to a platter; keep warm. Raise the heat to high and add the cornstarch and sesame oil. Stir continuously until the sauce thickens to a glaze. Pour the sauce over the vegetables and garnish with green onions. Serve hot.

NOTE: Fish puree is easy to make at home. Grind 1 pound of white fish fillets (flounder, halibut, black bass) until smooth in a food processor with 1 beaten egg white, 1 teaspoon salt, and 1 tablespoon cornstarch.

NONYA VEGETABLE CURRY

(*Nonya*)

This recipe exemplifies the Nonya cooking style. Coconut milk, Indian-style curry powder, lemongrass, turmeric, and tamarind are all ingredients that are traditional for the Malays but foreign to the Chinese. The vegetable selection reflects both the Chinese and Malay cultures. Serve this soup-like curry with rice. The recipe makes a large enough quantity for a large group or several meals.

Serves up to 12 with other dishes

6 ounces okra, trimmed
Vegetable oil for deep-frying
1 cup thickly sliced sweet potato (2 inches thick)
2 squares fresh firm tofu, cut in half diagonally and patted dry
2 Chinese eggplants, quartered lengthwise and cut into 2-inch lengths

REMPAH
5 candlenuts, soaked in water for 10 minutes, or skinless almonds
3 stalks fresh lemongrass, trimmed and sliced
8 shallots (walnut-size) or 2 medium onions, peeled and sliced
8 cloves garlic, peeled
1 teaspoon turmeric
½ cup vegetable oil
⅓ cup Red Chile Paste (see page 39)
1 tablespoon fresh or dried curry leaves, if available

✿

2 tablespoons Indian-style curry powder
1 can (13½ ounces) unsweetened coconut milk
1 cup water
⅔ cup tamarind water (see page 41)
1 tablespoon sugar
1½ teaspoons salt
1 cup large (1½-inch) cubes green cabbage
1 cup large (1½-inch) cubes purple cabbage
1 tomato, cut into wedges

1. Add 1 teaspoon of vegetable oil to a pot of water. Bring it to a boil and blanch the okra for 3 minutes; drain. Boil the sweet potato in fresh water until tender; drain.

2. Heat 2 inches of oil to 365°F in a wok or deep-fryer. Add the tofu and deep-fry until golden brown and crusty, about 3 minutes. Remove and drain. Deep-fry the eggplant strips for 2 to 3 minutes; remove and drain.

3. To make the *rempah*, grind the candlenuts, lemongrass, shallots, garlic, and turmeric into

a smooth paste in a blender or food processor. Add a tablespoon or more of water if needed to facilitate the blending. Heat the ½ cup of fresh oil in a wok or saucepan over low heat. Add the chile paste and curry leaves and fry, stirring continuously, until the oil takes on a reddish hue, about 2 minutes. Add the ground mixture and fry over low heat, stirring frequently, until the *rempah* is fragrant and has a rich mahogany-red color and a porridge-like consistency, about 8 minutes. It is ready when reddish oil seeps out.

4. Add the curry powder and coconut milk to the *rempah*. Bring it to a boil, stirring continuously. Reduce the heat and stir in the water, tamarind water, sugar, and salt. Add the vegetables and simmer until the vegetables are tender but crisp, about 8 minutes. Add the tomato just before serving.

FISH AND SHELLFISH

Fried Fish with Turmeric (*Acha Ikan Goreng*)
Fried Pomfret with Chile Sambal (*Sambal Ikan Goreng*)
Fish Curry with Okra, Tomato, and Mint (*Gulai Ikan*)
Grilled Fish in Banana Leaf Packets (*Otak Otak*)
Barbecued Whole Fish Wrapped in a Banana Leaf (*Ikan Panggang*)
Prawns Sauteed in Lemon-Chile Sambal (*Udang Goreng*)
Prawns Sauteed in Chile-Shallot Sambal (*Sambal Udang*)
Sauteed Squid with Spinach (Straits Chili Sotong)
Crunchy Fried Squid (*Sotong Goreng*)
Oyster Pancakes
Curry Crab
Chili Crab
Nonya Seafood Curry

Ikan Panggang (page 112)

ACHA IKAN GORENG

Fried Fish with Turmeric
(*Nonya*)

Acha Ikan Goreng is a Nonya wedding dish.

Serves 2 to 4 with other dishes

1 pomfret or trout (1 to 1½ pounds), dressed
¼ teaspoon salt, plus more for rubbing
Vegetable oil for frying
2-inch chunk fresh ginger, peeled and finely shredded
5 cloves garlic, peeled and sliced
1 teaspoon turmeric powder
½ cup white vinegar
3 tablespoons sugar
2 red jalapeño chiles, seeded and sliced lengthwise
Toasted sesame seeds, for garnish

1. Rinse the fish under cold water and pat dry. Make two diagonal slashes down to the bone on each side. Rub the fish with salt and set it aside.

2. Preheat a wok or deep frying pan. Add 2 to 2½ inches of oil and heat it to 365°F. Deep-fry the ginger until golden brown, about 1 minute. Lift it out with a strainer and drain on paper towels. Deep-fry the garlic until golden brown; drain.

3. Gently lower the fish into the hot oil. Deep-fry for 10 to 15 minutes or until golden brown, crisp, and dry. (The flesh should be almost flaky dry.) Drain on paper towels. Transfer to a serving plate and keep warm.

4. In a saucepan warm ¼ cup of fresh oil with the turmeric, vinegar, sugar, and ¼ teaspoon salt; cook over medium heat until the mixture begins to thicken, about 5 minutes. Add the chiles, ginger, and garlic and ladle the sauce over the fish. Garnish with sesame seeds. Serve warm or at room temperature.

SAMBAL IKAN GORENG

Fried Pomfret with Chile Sambal

(*Malay*)

Often in Singaporean-style cooking fish is deep-fried until the flesh is dry and flaky and the bones are cooked and crispy enough to eat. Pomfret, a popular fish in Southeast Asia, is the best choice for this recipe. If it is not available, use whole boneless rainbow trout, as the Straits Cafe does.

Serves 4 with other dishes

REMPAH
1 quarter-size slice fresh galangal, cut up (see Note, page 55)
1 stalk fresh lemongrass, trimmed and sliced
4 shallots (walnut-size) or 1 medium onion, peeled and sliced
3 cloves garlic, peeled and sliced
2 tablespoons vegetable oil
1 tablespoon Red Chile Paste (see page 39)

✿

1 tablespoon tamarind water (see page 41)
1 tablespoon sugar
¼ teaspoon salt, plus more for rubbing
1 whole pomfret or boneless trout, about 1½ pounds
Cornstarch
Vegetable oil for deep-frying
Fresh coriander leaves, for garnish
Cucumber slices, for garnish

1. To prepare the *rempah*, grind the galangal, lemongrass, shallots, and garlic to a smooth paste in a blender or food processor. Add a tablespoon or more of water if needed to facilitate the blending. Heat the oil in a wok or saucepan over medium heat. Add the chile paste and fry, stirring frequently, until the oil takes on a reddish hue, about 2 minutes. Add the ground mixture and fry, stirring frequently, until it is completely combined with the oil. Continue frying and stirring until the *rempah* is fragrant and has a mahogany-red color and a porridge-like consistency, about 5 minutes. When reddish oil seeps out, it is cooked. Stir in the tamarind water, sugar, and ¼ teaspoon salt. Keep warm.

2. Rinse the fish under cold water and pat it dry. Make two diagonal slashes down to the bone on each side. Rub the fish with salt and dust it lightly with cornstarch. Preheat a wok or deep frying pan. Add about 2 inches of oil and heat it to 365°F. Gently lower the fish into the hot oil and deep-fry for 10 to 15 minutes or until golden brown, crisp, and dry. (The flesh should be almost flaky dry.) Remove the fish and drain on paper towels. Transfer to a serving plate. Spread the chile sauce on both sides of the fish. Garnish with coriander and cucumber.

GULAI IKAN

Fish Curry with Okra, Tomato, and Mint
(*Nonya*)

The curry sauce in this recipe is luscious, sweet, tart, and spicy with the refreshing scent of mint and laksa leaves (see *daun kesom,* page 31). If laksa leaves are not available, do not try to substitute anything else. The curry will still be lively and peppery without them.

Mackerel is the traditional fish for this recipe. If you prefer, you may substitute tuna, swordfish, or catfish; they have plenty of depth to complement the richness of the sauce (see Note).

Serves 6

3½ cups tamarind water (see page 41)
¼ cup laksa leaves

REMPAH
4 candlenuts, soaked in water for 10 minutes, or skinless almonds
4 stalks fresh lemongrass, trimmed and sliced
6 shallots (walnut-size) or 1 large onion, peeled and sliced
10 cloves garlic, peeled
½-inch square (¼ inch thick) *blachan* (dried shrimp paste)
¼ cup vegetable oil
2 tablespoons Red Chile Paste (see page 39)

✿

1 teaspoon salt
3 tablespoons sugar
1 tomato, cut into cubes
6 okra, trimmed and boiled for 2 minutes
1 mackerel (1 to 1½ pounds), cleaned, head removed, cut crosswise into 1-inch-thick pieces
1 small handful mint leaves

1. Strain the tamarind water into a large saucepan. Add the laksa leaves and boil gently for 10 minutes. Keep warm.

2. To prepare the *rempah,* grind the candlenuts, lemongrass, shallots, garlic, and *blachan* to a smooth paste in a blender or food processor. Add a tablespoon or more of water if needed to facilitate the blending. Heat the oil in a wok or saucepan over medium heat. Add the chile paste and fry, stirring continuously, until the oil takes on a reddish hue, about 2 minutes. Add the ground mixture and fry over low heat, stirring frequently, until the *rempah* is fragrant and has a rich mahogany-red color and a porridge-like consistency, about 5 minutes. When reddish oil seeps out, it is ready. Add it to the tamarind water and simmer for 5 minutes. Season with salt and sugar. Add the tomato and okra; keep warm.

3. Boil the fish chunks in salted water for 3 minutes. Remove with a slotted spoon and add them to the saucepan. Garnish with mint. Serve with rice.

NOTE: Parboiling mackerel removes some of the excess oil and gives the fish a milder flavor. This step is unnecessary with leaner, milder fish; simply simmer them in the sauce until done.

OTAK OTAK

Grilled Fish in Banana Leaf Packets
(*Nonya*)

Asian cooks use banana, lotus, and bamboo leaves much as Americans use foil, to wrap, cook, and transport food. *Otak Otak* is a banana leaf packet of seasoned fish mousse which is steamed or, as in this recipe, grilled.

A popular snack, *Otak Otak* is a perfect picnic food because it serves well at room temperature. It's also a great barbecue dish because the wrapped fish cakes can be made in advance then grilled or broiled just before serving.

Makes 10

REMPAH
3 candlenuts, soaked in water for 10 minutes, or skinless almonds
3 stalks fresh lemongrass, trimmed and sliced
3 shallots (walnut-size) or 1 small onion, peeled and sliced
5 cloves garlic, peeled and sliced
3 red jalapeño chiles, stems removed
1 teaspoon turmeric powder
¼ teaspoon *blachan* (dried shrimp paste)

✿

1 cup unsweetened coconut milk (shake can well before opening)
1 tablespoon sugar
1 teaspoon salt
1 pound fresh fish puree (see Note)
1 tablespoon rice flour
1 egg, beaten
4 kaffir lime leaves (*daun limau perut*) or domestic lime leaves
10 banana leaves, cut into 7-inch squares

1. To make the *rempah,* grind the candlenuts, lemongrass, shallots, garlic, chiles, turmeric, and *blachan* to a smooth paste in a food processor. Add a tablespoon or more of water if needed to facilitate the blending.

2. Add the coconut milk, sugar, salt, fish puree, flour, and egg and process until thoroughly combined. With kitchen scissors, cut the lime leaves into extra-thin slivers; fold them into the fish mixture. You have made a fish mousse.

3. Wash the banana leaves in cold water. Dip the squares into boiling water for a minute to soften; remove and wipe them dry with a towel. Lay one square shiny side down with the lines running horizontally. Spread 2 to 3 tablespoons of mousse horizontally across the middle, leaving 1 inch free on both ends. Fold the top and bottom of the leaf over the mousse, overlapping them in the middle to form a packet. Flatten the packet evenly and seal the ends with toothpicks or short bamboo skewers. The packets may be prepared to this point and stored in the refrigerator for up to 4 hours. Allow them to come to room temperature before cooking.

4. Grill the packets over hot coals or broil them for 8 to 10 minutes, turning them once halfway through the cooking. To test for doneness, press the packets; they should feel firm.

NOTE: Mackerel is traditionally used in this dish. To make the fish puree at home, simply grind 1 pound of fillets in a food processor with 1 beaten egg white, 1 teaspoon salt, and 1 tablespoon cornstarch. You can substitute another white fish, or purchase a lightly seasoned fresh fish puree from an Asian fish market.

VARIATION: If you don't want to use banana leaves, you can spoon the fish mousse into ten ½-cup ramekins or custard cups and bake in a preheated 350°F oven for 15 minutes. Garnish with fresh coriander.

IKAN PANGGANG

Barbecued Whole Fish Wrapped in a Banana Leaf
(*Nonya*)

Barbecuing fish in a banana leaf is like baking it in foil—it keeps the fish succulent. We prefer the banana leaf because it infuses the fish with a herbaceous scent and flavor. This very easy recipe produces one of the tastiest fish dishes you'll ever eat. If banana leaves are not available, use foil.

Serves 2; serves 4 to 6 with other dishes

REMPAH
2 candlenuts, soaked in water for 10 minutes, or skinless almonds
1 stalk fresh lemongrass, trimmed and sliced
6 shallots (walnut-size) or 1 large onion, peeled and sliced
1 teaspoon *blachan* (dried shrimp paste)
2 fresh red jalapeño chiles or 6 fresh serrano chiles
3 kaffir lime leaves (*daun limau perut*)
1½ teaspoons sugar
1½ teaspoons salt

✿

2 whole pomfrets (10 ounces each) or 2 whole trout or 1 salmon trout (about 1½ pounds), dressed
Salt
2 pieces banana leaf or heavy-duty aluminum foil, 4 inches longer than and twice the width of the fish (1 piece if using salmon trout)
2 limes, cut into wedges
1 cucumber, cut into ½-inch cubes

1. To prepare the *rempah,* grind the candlenuts, lemongrass, shallots, *blachan,* and chiles to a smooth paste in a blender or food processor. Add a tablespoon or more of water if needed to facilitate the blending. Transfer the mixture to a bowl. Split the lime leaves in half lengthwise; tear off the spines and cut the leaves into fine slivers. Stir the leaves, sugar, and salt into the *rempah.* Set aside.

2. Scale the fish, rinse well with cold water, and pat thoroughly dry with paper towels. Cut off and discard the fins. Lay each fish flat on one side with its tail toward you. Cut a 1½-inch deep slit along the backbone, following the curve of the back from head to tail, to expose the backbone. Turn the fish over and repeat on the other side. (If the fish has a thin backbone, like trout, one slit will do.)

3. Season the fish with salt. Fill the slit and the cavity of each fish with the *rempah.* Dip the pieces of banana leaf in a pan of boiling water for a few seconds; wipe dry. Put the leaf shiny side down, place a fish on it, and fold the leaf over the fish. Seal the ends with bamboo skewers.

4. Prepare a charcoal fire. When the coals are glowing white, place the banana leaf packets over them on an oiled grill; cook for about 3 to 5 minutes on each side or until the fish are fully cooked. Remove the packets from the grill and unwrap the fish. Serve hot with rice garnished with lime wedges and cucumber cubes.

UDANG GORENG

Prawns Sauteed in Lemon-Chile Sambal
(*Malay*)

Asians love meat and fish cooked on the bone and shellfish in its shell. Shrimp cooked in the shell is far more flavorful and worth the extra work of removing the shells at the table. For a casual get-together such as a tailgate party, try serving *Udang Goreng* as an easy-to-prepare appetizer with beer.

Serves 4 to 6

½ pound large shrimp (26 to 30 per pound) in the shell
1 tablespoon vegetable oil
1 teaspoon chopped garlic
1 tablespoon Thai fish sauce
1 tablespoon Red Chile Paste (see page 39)
Juice of ¼ lemon
1 tablespoon sugar

1. Pat the shrimp dry. With kitchen shears make a cut about an inch long through each shell along the shrimp's round dorsal curve (back). If you can see a black vein, grasp it with your finger tips and gently draw it out; discard.

2. Heat a wok over medium-high heat. Add the oil and garlic and stir-fry until light golden brown. Increase the heat to high. Add the shrimp. Spread them out so that the shells become crisp and browned. Cook about 1 minute, tossing occasionally. When they turn bright orange, add the fish sauce, chile paste, lemon juice, and sugar. Toss together until the sauce glazes the shrimp. Transfer to a serving dish and serve hot or at room temperature.

VARIATION: *Udang Goreng* can be made with tamarind instead of lemon. Marinate the shrimp in ½ cup of tamarind water before stir-frying.

SAMBAL UDANG

Prawns Sauteed in Chile-Shallot Sambal
(*Malay*)

The Straits Cafe served this at a dinner for the International Wine and Food Society; its members declared it their favorite dish in the 8-course meal. It is a classic Malaysian recipe, in which shrimp are lightly sauteed in a shallot-chile sambal and finished with a touch of lime juice.

Sambal Udang is a natural accompaniment for Nasi Lemak (page 83), fragrant rice simmered in coconut milk. Complete this meal with a green salad.

Serves 3 to 4

REMPAH
1 quarter-size slice fresh galangal, cut up (see Note, page 55)
2 candlenuts, soaked in water for 10 minutes, or skinless almonds
1 stalk fresh lemongrass, trimmed and sliced
4 shallots (walnut-size) or 1 medium onion, peeled and sliced
3 cloves garlic, peeled and sliced
½-inch square (¼ inch thick) *blachan* (dried shrimp paste)
¼ cup vegetable oil
2 tablespoons Red Chile Paste (see page 39)

✿

¾ pound large shrimp (26 to 30 per pound), shelled and deveined
1 small onion, sliced
1 tomato, cut into wedges
2 tablespoons sugar
1 teaspoon salt
1 tablespoon fresh lime juice

1. To prepare the *rempah*, grind the galangal, candlenuts, lemongrass, shallots, garlic, and *blachan* to a smooth paste in a blender or food processor. Add a tablespoon or more of water if needed to facilitate the blending. Heat the oil in a wok or saucepan over medium heat. Carefully add the chile paste and fry for 2 minutes, stirring continuously, until the oil takes on a reddish hue. Add the ground mixture and fry, stirring frequently, until the *rempah* is fragrant and has a dark mahogany-red color and a porridge-like consistency, about 5 minutes. It is ready when reddish oil seeps out.

2. Toss the shrimp, onion, and tomato into the *rempah*; stir-fry over high heat until the shrimp turn bright orange and feel firm to the touch, about 2 minutes. Season with sugar, salt, and lime juice. Serve hot with *Nasi Lemak*.

STRAITS CHILI SOTONG

Sauteed Squid with Spinach

(*Straits Cafe*)

This recipe can be served as one of many in an Asian menu or as a side dish in a Western menu. Already cleaned fresh squid is available in better seafood markets; the price is worth the savings in time and work. It is important that the squid is cooked quickly; any longer than 2 minutes and it will turn rubbery.

Serves 4 to 5

¾ pound cleaned squid bodies and tentacles
2 tablespoons vegetable oil
1 tablespoon chopped garlic
8 dried hot red chiles
¼ cup Chinese rice wine
¼ cup oyster sauce
½ tablespoon sugar
1 teaspoon cornstarch dissolved in 2 teaspoons water
Asian sesame oil, to taste
1 pound spinach, blanched or stir-fried

1. Rinse the squid with cold water. Thoroughly pat them dry. Cut the tubes into ½- to 1-inch rings; set aside.

2. Heat a wok over medium heat. Add the oil. Add the garlic and saute until golden brown. Increase the heat to high. Add the chiles and squid; quickly stir-fry until the squid turns opaque. Immediately add the rice wine, oyster sauce, and sugar. (If there is excess liquid pour off all but a few tablespoons.) Stir in the cornstarch and toss quickly to thicken the sauce into a glaze. Swirl in the sesame oil. Arrange the squid over the spinach and serve hot.

SOTONG GORENG

Crunchy Fried Squid
(*Nonya*)

This recipe is unusual in that the squid is deep-fried without a batter or flour coating. When each piece is completely dry and crunchy, the squid is tossed with a simmered glaze of Chinese hoisin sauce, rice wine, and sugar. *Sotong Goreng* makes a delicious, irresistible appetizer with beer.

Serves 4 to 8 as an appetizer

1½ pounds cleaned squid tubes and tentacles
Vegetable oil, for deep-frying

HOISIN SAUCE GLAZE
1 tablespoon vegetable oil
¼ cup hoisin sauce
2 tablespoons rice wine
3 tablespoons sugar

✿

Toasted sesame seeds, for garnish

1. Thoroughly rinse the squid with cold water and pat dry. Cut the tubes into ½-inch rings.

2. Preheat a wok and pour 2 to 2½ inches of oil into it, or pour the oil into a deep-fryer. Heat the oil to 365°F. Add the squid and deep-fry until golden brown, crisp, and dry, about 7 to 8 minutes. Take one piece out and try it; it should be crunchy like a potato chip. Drain the squid on paper towels, then transfer to a bowl.

3. Combine 1 tablespoon of fresh oil with the hoisin sauce, wine, and sugar in a saucepan; cook and stir until the sugar dissolves. Allow the glaze to cool, then toss the squid in it until each piece is coated. Sprinkle with sesame seeds. Serve at room temperature.

OYSTER PANCAKES
(*Chinese*)

Oyster Pancakes are among the most popular dishes at the hawker centers in Singapore. Once you taste them, you crave them. In this Asian "omelette," oysters are stir-fried with chopped garlic, Chinese (garlic) chives, seasonings, and eggs. The tiny oysters found there are about the same size as Olympia oysters and are used whole; larger American oysters need to be cut up. Fresh shucked oysters are best, but jarred oysters will also work well in this recipe. Try Oyster Pancakes with toasted garlic croutons for a delicious Western-style brunch.

Serves 4 with other dishes

5 large fresh oysters or ½ jar oysters (about 5)
1 tablespoon water chestnut powder
2 tablespoons cornstarch
1 tablespoon oyster sauce
½ teaspoon sugar
⅛ teaspoon white pepper
3 tablespoons water
2 tablespoons Chinese chives or green onions, cut into ¼-inch lengths
2 tablespoons vegetable oil
2 teaspoons chopped garlic
2 eggs, lightly beaten
2 tablespoons fish sauce
1 tablespoon sriracha sauce

1. Cut the oysters into thirds; set aside.

2. In a bowl combine the water chestnut powder, cornstarch, oyster sauce, sugar, pepper, and water; stir into a smooth paste. Add the oysters, chives, and 1 tablespoon of oil.

3. Heat the remaining tablespoon of oil in a large skillet or on a griddle. Saute the garlic over medium heat until light golden brown. Raise the heat to medium-high. Pour in the oyster mixture and spread it out in a single layer. Gently stir and turn the mixture so that all the uncooked parts reach the bottom of the pan. When it begins to brown, about 1 to 2 minutes, pour the eggs over the oyster mixture. Fold the eggs and oysters together (as if you were folding beaten egg whites into a soufflé batter), breaking up large chunks of the oyster pancake and turning them over into a loose omelette. The omelette is finished when the eggs are cooked but still moist. Serve with the fish sauce and sriracha sauce.

CURRY CRAB
(*Indian/Chinese*)

A truly cross-cultural recipe, this dish reflects both Chinese and Indian influences. Cooking crab in its shell to bring out its flavor is a popular Chinese technique. The crab is then simmered in an Indian-style curry sauce spiked with exotic spices, cinnamon, and cloves and tempered by coconut milk. Have a finger bowl ready for each diner.

Serves 2; serves 4 to 6 with other dishes

1 live crab, about 2 to 2½ pounds (preferably Dungeness)

REMPAH
4 candlenuts, soaked in water for 10 minutes, or skinless almonds
2 stalks fresh lemongrass, trimmed and sliced
1-inch chunk fresh ginger, peeled and cut up
4 shallots (walnut-size) or 1 medium onion, peeled and sliced
6 cloves garlic, peeled and sliced
½ teaspoon turmeric powder

✿

Vegetable oil for deep-frying
½ cup vegetable oil
3 cinnamon sticks
1 teaspoon whole cloves
12 whole cardamom pods
2 sprigs fresh curry leaves or 1 tablespoon dried curry leaves
⅓ cup Red Chile Paste (see page 39)
2 tablespoons Indian-style curry powder
1 can (13½ ounces) unsweetened coconut milk, shaken well
1 tablespoon sugar
1½ teaspoons salt

1. Clean, kill, and cut up the crab (see steps 1 and 2, page 120). Set aside.

2. To prepare the *rempah*, grind the candlenuts, lemongrass, ginger, shallots, and garlic to a smooth paste in a blender or food processor. Add a tablespoon or more of water if needed to facilitate the blending. Transfer the mixture to a bowl, mix in the turmeric, and set aside.

3. Heat 2 to 3 inches of oil to 365°F in a wok or deep-fryer. Add the crab a few pieces at a time and deep-fry for 1 minute to brown the edges. Remove and drain.

4. Heat ½ cup of oil in a wok over medium-high heat. Add the cinnamon sticks, cloves, cardamom pods, curry leaves, and chile paste. Fry for about 2 minutes, stirring continuously, then add the *rempah*. Fry, stirring frequently, until the *rempah* is completely combined with the oil and has a creamy porridge-like consistency, about 5 to 7 minutes. When reddish oil seeps out of the mixture, stir in the curry powder, coconut milk, sugar, and salt. Add the fried crab and simmer for about 5 minutes. Serve hot with rice.

CHILI CRAB

(*Singapore*)

Chili Crab is one of the national dishes of Singapore. Everyone who makes a trip to Singapore should try this famous stir-fried crab in the shell with a spicy sweet-and-sour tomato sauce.

Serves 2; serves 4 to 6 with other dishes

1 live crab, preferably Dungeness, about 2 to 2½ pounds
Oil for deep-frying
1 tablespoon chopped garlic
½ cup chicken stock
1 tablespoon Thai fish sauce
1 tablespoon sriracha sauce or Red Chile Paste **(see page 39)**
4 tablespoons ketchup
3 tablespoons sugar
1½ teaspoons salt
2 eggs
Swirl of Asian sesame oil
1 green onion, including top, chopped

1. Put the crab in the sink and rinse it under cold water. With a long-handled brush, scrub the underside and between the claws and legs (watch out for those claws!) to remove any sand and grit. Rinse thoroughly. Kill the crab—I do it by plunging it into boiling water for 1 minute.

2. To disjoint and crack the crab, lift the triangular apron on the underside with the tip of a knife. Grasp the apron and lift and twist it off. The intestinal tube should come out with it. Hold the top shell in one hand while gathering all the legs and claws with the other hand. Gently rock the legs back and forth to separate the shell from the body; pull away the shell. Pull off and discard the feathery gills on each side of the body and the mandibles at the "face" end. Now gently bend the legs and claws backward and twist them free. You are left with the chest section, with the creamy yellow tomalley (greenish in an uncooked crab) in the center. Spoon the tomalley out and reserve it for those who appreciate it. Chop the chest down the center with a cleaver, then cut each half crosswise into three equal pieces. Crack each leg and claw at the joint and in the middle with a light hammer or nutcracker.

3. Preheat a wok. Add 2 to 3 inches of oil and heat it to 365°F. Add the crab a few pieces at a time and deep-fry for 1 minute to brown the edges. Remove and drain thoroughly. Pour off or ladle all but 1 tablespoon of the oil into a safe container to be discarded.

4. Heat the wok with the remaining oil over medium heat. Add the garlic and stir-fry until lightly golden brown. Increase the heat to high. Add the crab pieces and toss them vigorously for 1 minute. Pour in the chicken stock, fish sauce, sriracha sauce, ketchup, sugar, and salt. Bring to a boil while tossing and stirring the crab vigorously. Crack the eggs into the wok; toss quickly, breaking up the eggs. As they cook the sauce will thicken into a glaze. Swirl the sesame oil over

the mixture. This whole stir-frying process should take no longer than 5 minutes. Transfer to a platter; if you like, assemble the legs and claws on the serving platter in a lifelike pattern and place the shell on top (see photo). Spoon any remaining sauce over the crab and garnish with green onion. Serve with rice.

VARIATION: If you prefer not to deep-fry the crab, eliminate the deep-frying step and let the crab simmer in the sauce, covered, for 8 to 10 minutes or until cooked. During the last 1 minute of cooking crack the eggs into the wok and stir-fry until they are set.

NONYA SEAFOOD CURRY

(*Nonya*)

This soup-like curry contains a rich and luxurious assortment of seafood, vegetables, and herbs. *Daun limau perut* (also known as kaffir lime leaf) adds a distinctive citrus flavor and perfume. Although the American lime pales next to the Asian lime, it may be substituted. Serve as a light supper with steamed rice or crusty bread.

Serves 4

REMPAH
1 teaspoon cumin seeds
2 teaspoons coriander seeds
1 quarter-size slice fresh galangal, cut up (see Note, page 55)
2 stalks fresh lemongrass, trimmed and sliced
4 shallots (walnut-size) or 1 onion, peeled and sliced
4 cloves garlic, peeled and sliced
3 fresh red jalapeño chiles, seeded
1 teaspoon *blachan* (dried shrimp paste)
Roots of 8 fresh coriander plants, if available
¼ cup vegetable oil
2 kaffir lime leaves (*daun limau perut*)

✿

1 can (13½ ounces) unsweetened coconut milk plus ½ can water
1 teaspoon sugar
¾ teaspoon salt
1 Chinese eggplant
1 cup sliced bamboo shoots

8 fresh mussels
½ pound large shrimp (26 to 30 per pound), shelled and deveined
½ pound fresh cleaned squid with tentacles, cut into 1-inch rings

1. To prepare the *rempah,* grind the cumin and coriander seeds to a powder in a spice mill or mortar; set aside. Grind the galangal, lemongrass, shallots, garlic, chiles, *blachan,* and coriander roots to a smooth paste in a blender or food processor. Add a tablespoon or more of water if needed to facilitate the blending.

2. Heat the oil in a wok or saucepan over medium heat. Carefully add the shallot mixture and fry, stirring frequently, until it is completely combined with the oil. Continue frying and stirring until the *rempah* is porridge-like in consistency and fragrant, about 5 minutes. Finely shred the lime leaves; add them and the ground seeds. Cook 1 minute longer. Add the coconut milk, water, sugar, and salt; simmer for 5 minutes.

3. Cut the eggplant lengthwise into quarters and then crosswise into 2-inch lengths. Add the eggplant and bamboo shoots to the wok. Simmer until tender, about 5 minutes. Meanwhile, debeard the mussels and scrub the shells under running cold water. Increase the heat to medium-high; add the shrimp and mussels. Cook until the mussels open up, about a minute or 2. Thirty seconds before the cooking is done, add the squid. Serve hot.

POULTRY

Spicy Chicken
with Fragrant Lime Sauce
(*Ayam Kalasan*)
Fried Chicken with Salt Fish
(*Ayam Goreng*)
Fried Chicken in Tomato Sauce
and Mint (*Ayam Goreng Pedas*)
Barbecued Cornish Hens (*Ayam Panggang*)
Braised Chicken Thighs Nonya
Style (*Ayam Sioh*)
Aromatic Braised Chicken in
Turmeric (*Ayam Kunyit*)
Basil Chicken (*Ayam Basil*)
Hainanese Chicken Rice
Chicken in "Dry" Curry Sauce
(*Ayam Rendang*)
Sweet and Lemony Chicken
Thighs (*Ayam Kapitan*)
Mild Coconut Chicken Curry
(*Patong Ayam*)

Ayam Panggang (page 130)

AYAM KALASAN

Spicy Fried Chicken with Fragrant Lime Sauce
(*Malay*)

Some dishes are worth every step in their production; this is one. Traditionally *Ayam Kalasan* is double deep-fried; however, the final frying can be replaced by broiling or grilling.

This recipe makes enough sauce for two chickens. If you want to cook only one chicken, still make the full sauce recipe; it is best when made in a large quantity and it does freeze well.

Serves 4

2 chickens, 2½ pounds each
Vegetable oil for deep-frying

REMPAH
2 quarter-size slices fresh galangal, cut up (see Note, page 55)
6 candlenuts, soaked in water for 10 minutes, or skinless almonds
6 stalks fresh lemongrass, trimmed and sliced
8 shallots (walnut-size) or 2 medium onions, peeled and sliced
10 cloves garlic, peeled and sliced
8 red jalapeño chiles, stems removed
1 teaspoon turmeric powder
½ cup vegetable oil

✿

1 can (13½ ounces) unsweetened coconut milk
10 kaffir lime leaves (*daun limau perut*) or fresh lime leaves, finely shredded
2 teaspoons salt
2 tablespoons sugar
Mint leaves, for garnish
2 lemons, cut into wedges

1. Cut each chicken into 10 pieces; pat dry. Preheat a wok. Pour in 2 to 3 inches of oil and heat it to 365°F. Deep-fry a few pieces of chicken at a time until golden brown, about 8 minutes. Drain on paper towels. Set aside the wok and oil to be used later.

2. To prepare the *rempah*, grind the galangal, candlenuts, lemongrass, shallots, garlic, chiles, and turmeric to a smooth paste in a blender or food processor. Add a tablespoon or more of water if needed to facilitate the blending. Heat the ½ cup of oil in a wok or saucepan over medium heat. Add the ground mixture and fry, stirring frequently, until it is completely mixed with the oil. Continue frying until the *rempah* is fragrant and has a light orange color and porridge-like consistency, about 8 minutes. It is ready when oil seeps out.

3. Add the coconut milk, lime leaves, salt, and sugar. Cook, stirring, for 1 minute. Continue cooking over medium heat, stirring frequently, until the mixture becomes creamy, about 2 minutes.

Add the fried chicken and simmer until oil peeks through the mixture, about 5 minutes. Remove the chicken from the sauce, scraping off any excess sauce.

4. Reheat the deep-frying oil to 365°F. Deep-fry the chicken pieces, a few at a time, until crisp and golden brown, about 2 minutes. Drain on paper towels. Arrange the chicken on a serving platter and pour the sauce on top. Garnish with mint leaves and lemon wedges.

AYAM GORENG
Fried Chicken with Salt Fish
(*Straits Cafe*)

Deep-fried chicken is universally popular and each country has its version. This Nonya-style fried chicken is by far one of the most interesting and tasty.

[American cooks may hesitate to try this dish if you are not familiar with Asian sun-dried fish. But I am certain you will like Chris's version, which is simple to prepare and alive with delicious sweet-salty flavors. I think one needs to cultivate one's mind rather than a taste for this unique sweet-salt flavor. Think of Asian dried salted fish in the same light as the respected salt cod of Europe—Spanish bacalao, *Italian* baccala, *and French* morue. *It is used in the same way to season a dish.—J.J.]*

Serves 4 to 6

1½ ounces dried salt fish
Vegetable oil for deep-frying
1 chicken (2½ pounds), cut into parts
1 teaspoon white pepper
2 tablespoons sugar
3 tablespoons oyster sauce
3 tablespoons Chinese rice wine or white wine
3 tablespoons Asian sesame oil

1. Slice the salt fish diagonally into thin slivers. Half-fill a wok or large deep pan with oil. Heat the oil to 365°F. Add the salt fish and fry it until golden brown, less than a minute. Drain it on paper towels. When cool, grind it into a fine powder.

2. Toss the chicken pieces with the powdered fish in a bowl. Mix the remaining ingredients in a separate bowl and pour them over the chicken. Marinate for 2 hours or longer.

3. Reheat the oil to 365°F. Add the chicken pieces (watch out for splatters) and deep-fry until golden brown and done, about 8 to 10 minutes. Drain and serve hot.

AYAM GORENG PEDAS

Fried Chicken in Tomato Sauce and Mint
(*Malay*)

This unusual fried chicken is served in a refreshing mildly spicy tomato sauce with a touch of mint. Serve it with steamed rice and a light soup to complete the meal.

Serves 4 to 6

1 chicken (2½ pounds), cut into parts
½ teaspoon salt
½ teaspoon turmeric powder
Vegetable oil for deep-frying

REMPAH
5 dried red California or New Mexico chiles
5 small fresh red Thai or serrano chiles, stems and seeds removed
2 stalks fresh lemongrass, trimmed and sliced
4 shallots (walnut-size) or 1 medium onion, peeled and sliced
6 cloves garlic, peeled and sliced
¼ cup vegetable oil

✿

4 tablespoons tomato ketchup
1 tablespoon white vinegar
4 teaspoons sugar
1 teaspoon salt
¼ cup diced cooked carrots
¼ cup peas
20 fresh mint leaves

1. Rub the chicken with salt and turmeric. Preheat a wok. Add 2 to 3 inches of oil and heat to 365°F. Deep-fry the chicken pieces a few at a time until golden brown, about 8 minutes. Drain on paper towels. Set aside.

2. Meanwhile prepare the *rempah:* Cut off and discard the stems from the dried chiles. Shake loose and discard the seeds. Put the dried chiles in a saucepan; cover them with water and bring to a boil. Cook at a low boil until soft, about 5 minutes. Drain. Put the chiles into a blender or mini-food processor with the fresh chiles; grind them into a puree. Transfer to a bowl; set aside.

3. Grind the lemongrass, shallots, and garlic to a smooth paste in a blender or food processor. Add a tablespoon or more of water if needed to facilitate the blending; set aside.

4. Heat the ¼ cup of oil in a wok or saucepan over medium heat. Add the chile puree and fry, stirring continuously, until the oil takes on a reddish hue, about 2 minutes. Add the ground mixture and fry, stirring frequently, until it is completely combined with the oil. Continue frying

until the *rempah* is fragrant and has a deep mahogany-red color and porridge-like consistency, about 8 minutes. It is ready when reddish oil seeps out. Stir in the ketchup and vinegar and season with sugar and salt. Add the chicken, carrots, and peas; cook 1 minute longer. Fold in the mint leaves and serve.

AYAM PANGGANG
Barbecued Cornish Hens
(*Malay*)

Not only is this simple to make, it is one of the best barbecued poultry recipes you'll ever have. The sauce is aromatic, rich, and mildly spiced with the tangy taste of lime. Although the oil is necessary for cooking the *rempah*, after the sauce is finished you may spoon the extra oil off and discard it. Traditionally, chicken is used in this recipe, but we found that cornish hens are fabulous done this way.

Serves 6

6 cornish hens (or 3 small broiler chickens)

REMPAH
10 kaffir lime leaves (*daun limau perut*) or fresh lime leaves
6 candlenuts, soaked in water for 10 minutes, or skinless almonds
5 stalks fresh lemongrass, trimmed and sliced
10 shallots (walnut-size) or 2 onions, peeled and sliced
10 cloves garlic, peeled and sliced
8 red jalapeño chiles, stems removed
1 teaspoon turmeric powder

✿

1 can (13½ ounces) coconut milk, shaken well
3 tablespoons sugar
1 tablespoon salt
⅓ cup vegetable oil
1 lime, cut into wedges

1. Cut the hens (or chickens) in half lengthwise. With a fork, pierce the birds all over; set them aside in a large, deep bowl.

2. To make the *rempah*, fold the lime leaves in half and tear off the center spines. Cut the leaves

into very fine shreds; set aside. Grind the candlenuts, lemongrass, shallots, garlic, chiles, and turmeric to a smooth paste in a blender or food processor. Add a tablespoon or more of water if needed to facilitate the blending. Transfer the *rempah* to a large bowl. Add the coconut milk, sugar, salt, and lime leaf shreds; mix thoroughly. You should have about 3½ cups. Pour 1½ cups over the birds; marinate for at least 30 minutes. Reserve the remaining *rempah*.

3. Preheat the oven to 450°F. Remove the hens from the *rempah*, scraping off the excess (combine it with the reserved *rempah*). Set the hens skin side up on a baking sheet. Bake the hens for 15 minutes (chickens for 20 minutes). Turn off the oven but leave the birds 5 minutes longer.

4. While the hens bake, set a wok over medium heat. Heat the ⅓ cup of oil. Add the *rempah* and fry, stirring frequently, until it is combined completely with the oil. Continue frying until the mixture is fragrant and has a medium orange color and a porridge-like consistency, about 8 minutes. It is ready when orange oil seeps out.

5. Heat the barbecue or grill. When the coals are glowing red, barbecue the birds for 3 minutes on each side until golden brown. Pour the *rempah* over the birds. Serve hot with a squeeze of lime.

AYAM SIOH

Braised Chicken Thighs Nonya Style
(*Nonya*)

This braised chicken is infused with the savory and herbaceous taste of lesser ginger (see page 35), a medicinal rhizome related to ginger. Don't skip the parboiling step before braising the chicken or the dish will end up with an unpleasant scum and dull color.

Serves 6 with other dishes

6 chicken thighs
6 shallots (walnut-size) or 1 large onion, peeled and sliced
12 cloves garlic, peeled and sliced
½ cup vegetable oil
1 tablespoon *tau cheo* (yellow bean sauce), chopped
1 tablespoon ground coriander seeds
1½ teaspoons lesser ginger powder
1 teaspoon white pepper
1 cup water
1 teaspoon dark soy sauce
3½ tablespoons sugar
1 teaspoon salt
½ teaspoon Asian sesame oil
Chopped green onions, for garnish
Crisp Shallot Flakes (page 166)
Sliced fresh red chiles, for garnish

1. Bring a large pot of water to a boil. Add the chicken and bring to a second boil. Boil 1 minute or until scum rises to the surface. Drain; set the chicken aside.

2. Grind the shallots and garlic to a smooth paste in a blender or food processor. Add a tablespoon or more of water if needed to facilitate the blending.

3. Heat the ½ cup of oil in a wok or saucepan over medium heat. Add the shallot mixture and saute lightly, without browning, until thick. Add the bean sauce; stir-fry for 1 minute. Add the coriander, lesser ginger, and white pepper; cook until the mixture is khaki color, about 1 minute. Add the chicken, water, soy sauce, sugar, and salt; stir together and simmer for 15 minutes. Mix in the sesame oil. Transfer to a platter and garnish with green onions, shallot flakes, and chiles. Serve with rice.

AYAM KUNYIT

Aromatic Braised Chicken in Turmeric
(*Nonya*)

Ayam Kunyit is a braised chicken dish which combines the seasonings of India with the cooking techniques of Malaysia. Tamarind accents the dish with its unique citrus taste.

Serves 4 to 6 with other dishes

1 chicken (2½ pounds), cut into parts

REMPAH
1-inch piece fresh galangal, peeled and sliced (see Note, page 55)
5 stalks lemongrass, trimmed and sliced
10 cloves garlic, peeled
10 shallots (walnut-size) or 2 onions, peeled
1 tablespoon turmeric powder
¼ cup vegetable oil

✿

5 curry leaves, preferably fresh
3 stalks lemongrass, trimmed and slapped with the side of a cleaver
2 tablespoons Indian-style curry powder
1 teaspoon brown mustard seeds
1 can (13½ ounces) coconut milk, shaken well
1½ cups tamarind water (see page 41)
1 teaspoon salt
1 tablespoon sugar
2 red or green jalapeño chiles, stemmed, seeded, and thinly sliced lengthwise
½ onion, cut into wedges
1 tomato, cut into 8 chunks

1. Bring a large pot of water to a boil. Add the chicken and bring the water to a second boil. Boil the chicken for 1 minute or until scum rises to the surface. Drain the chicken and set it aside.

2. To make the *rempah,* grind the galangal, sliced lemongrass, garlic, shallots, and turmeric to a smooth paste in a blender or food processor. Add a tablespoon or more of water if needed to facilitate the blending. Heat the ¼ cup of oil in a wok or saucepan over medium heat. Add the curry leaves and the ground mixture. Fry, stirring frequently, until the *rempah* is completely combined with the oil. Continue frying until the mixture is fragrant and has a porridge-like consistency, about 5 minutes. It is ready when orange oil seeps out. Add the lemongrass stalks, curry powder, mustard seeds, coconut milk, tamarind water, and chicken pieces and cook, uncovered, for 10 minutes. Season with the salt and sugar. Cook 5 minutes, then add the chiles, onion, and tomato. Cook 5 minutes longer. Discard the lemongrass stalks. Serve hot with rice.

AYAM BASIL

Basil Chicken

(*Malay*)

This stew-like dish intermingles boneless chicken and vegetables with a refreshing lemon-basil sauce.

Serves 4 to 6, with other dishes

4 dried Chinese black mushrooms
1 pound boneless chicken breast or thighs

REMPAH
5 candlenuts, soaked in water for 10 minutes, or skinless almonds
5 stalks fresh lemongrass, trimmed and sliced
4 shallots (walnut-size) or 1 medium onion, peeled and sliced
6 cloves garlic, peeled and sliced
10 red serrano chiles, stems removed
Roots and stems from ½ bunch fresh coriander
1 teaspoon turmeric powder
4 tablespoons vegetable oil

✿

¼ cup cooked carrots, cut in ¼-inch dice
1 can (13½ ounces) unsweetened coconut milk, shaken well
½ onion, cut into ¼-inch-thick slices
¼ cup peas
½ cup bamboo shoot strips
3 tablespoons sugar
1 teaspoon salt
Juice of 1 lemon
⅓ cup fresh basil leaves
1 fresh red jalapeño chile, sliced lengthwise
Cooked rice

1. Cover the mushrooms with water and let them soak for 30 minutes or until soft and pliable. Cut off and discard the stems; cut the caps into slices; set aside.

2. Remove the skin from the chicken. Cut the meat into ½-inch strips and set aside.

3. To prepare the *rempah*, grind the candlenuts, lemongrass, shallots, garlic, chiles, coriander roots and stems, and turmeric to a smooth paste in a blender or food processor. Add a tablespoon or more of water if needed to facilitate the blending. Heat the oil in a wok or saucepan over medium heat. Add the ground mixture and fry, stirring frequently, until the *rempah* is fragrant and has a light orange color and a porridge-like consistency, about 8 minutes. It is ready when oil seeps out.

4. Increase the heat to medium-high. Toss in the chicken, carrots, and coconut milk. Stir continuously until the mixture comes to a boil. Reduce to a lively simmer and add the mushrooms, onion, peas, bamboo shoots, sugar, salt, and lemon juice. Cook for 1 minute or until the chicken feels firm to the touch. Add the basil and cook until it wilts. Garnish with the chile slices. Serve hot with rice.

HAINANESE CHICKEN RICE

(China)

Chicken rice is one of Singapore's signature dishes, and one Joyce has every time she visits. The dish consists of four parts: poached chicken, aromatic chicken-flavored rice, a light soup with Chinese vegetables, and three dipping sauces—sesame-soy sauce, sweet chili sauce, and gingered oil dipping sauce. Traditionally, the chicken is hacked, that is, cut up Chinese style with skin and bones attached. If you prefer, you may serve the meat boned, as the Straits Cafe does.

Serves 2 as lunch or 4 to 6 for dinner with other dishes

HAINANESE CHICKEN
1 fresh chicken (2½ pounds)
1 teaspoon salt
5 quarts water
4 1-inch chunks ginger, slapped with the side of a cleaver

AROMATIC CHICKEN-FLAVORED RICE
2 cups long-grain rice
3 tablespoons vegetable oil (optional)
1 tablespoon finely minced peeled ginger
5 cloves garlic, peeled and finely minced
1 tablespoon Asian sesame oil
2½ cups chicken stock (from Step 2, if desired)
1 teaspoon salt
1 pandan leaf (optional), tied into a knot

DIPPING SAUCES
Sesame-Soy Dipping Sauce (see page 159)
Chile-Ginger Sambal (see page 160)
Gingered Oil Dipping Sauce (see page 159)

✿

2 cups Chinese cabbage in 1-inch dice
2 green onions, chopped
1 cucumber, peeled and cut into ¼-inch slices, for garnish
Fresh coriander leaves

1. Remove the fat from the chicken cavity and set it aside. Rub the chicken thoroughly inside and out with the 1 teaspoon of salt; set aside for 1 hour. If you want to use the chicken fat to cook the rice (step 3), put it in a small saucepan; cook on medium-low heat to render 3 tablespoons of fat. Set aside.

2. Bring the water and ginger to a boil in a stockpot. Add the chicken. Bring to a second boil and skim off and discard the scum that rises to the surface. If the chicken is not entirely submerged, add enough water to cover it. Cover the pot, reduce the heat, and simmer for 20 minutes. Carefully remove the chicken to a large bowl filled with cold water; set aside and allow the chicken to cool. Keep the stock warm. When the chicken is cool, drain it and set aside. (If you are not continuing with the recipe right away, refrigerate both the chicken and the stock. Reheat the stock to continue the recipe.)

3. To make the aromatic chicken-flavored rice, put the rice in a large bowl and rinse it with cold water until the water runs clear. Drain thoroughly. Heat the rendered chicken fat, or oil if you prefer, in a medium saucepan over medium heat. Add the ginger and garlic and saute lightly until aromatic, about 1 minute. Do not brown. Add the drained rice and sesame oil; saute for 1 minute. Add 2½ cups of chicken stock and salt. Boil over high heat until there is no water left on the surface of the rice. Place the pandan leaf on top. Cover the pot, reduce the heat, and simmer until steam no longer seeps through the cover, about 10 minutes. Turn off the heat and allow the rice to stand for another 10 minutes; do not remove the cover. Meanwhile, prepare the dipping sauces.

4. To serve, chop the chicken Chinese-style into bite-size pieces with the skin and bone attached. If serving lunch for two, divide the chicken between two plates; otherwise, arrange the pieces on a platter. Keep it covered until ready to serve. Strain the remaining chicken stock into a pot and bring it to a boil. Add the Chinese cabbage. When it begins to wilt, serve about 1 cup of soup with cabbage per person. Sprinkle the green onions on top. Garnish the chicken plate with cucumber slices and coriander leaves and serve with a bowl of hot aromatic chicken-flavored rice and the dipping sauces.

AYAM RENDANG

Chicken in "Dry" Curry Sauce
(*Malay*)

Here is a great chicken dish that can be made in advance and reheated. The curry-flavored sauce is simmered slowly until it becomes a "dry" coating for the chicken. It is important not to rush the cooking; the chicken needs time to absorb the flavors of the *rempah.* Beef or lamb *rendang* is delicious, too, and very popular in Singapore.

Serves 4 with other dishes

1 chicken (2½ pounds), quartered

REMPAH
5 dried red California or New Mexico chiles
5 small red fresh Thai or serrano chiles
6 quarter-size slices fresh galangal, cut up (see Note, page 55)
6 candlenuts, soaked in water for 10 minutes, or skinless almonds
4 stalks fresh lemongrass, trimmed and sliced
10 shallots (walnut-size) or 2 onions, peeled and sliced
6 cloves garlic, peeled and sliced
½ cup vegetable oil

✿

3 stalks fresh lemongrass, slapped with the side of a cleaver
1 can (13½ ounces) unsweetened coconut milk, shaken well
1 tablespoon sugar
½ tablespoon salt
1 cup grated unsweetened coconut, toasted

1. Bring a large pot of water to a boil. Add the chicken and bring the water to a second boil. Boil for 1 minute or until scum rises to the surface. Drain the chicken and set it aside.

2. To prepare the *rempah,* cut off and discard the stems from the dried chiles. Shake loose and discard the seeds. Put the seeded chiles in a saucepan and cover them with water; bring to a boil. Cook at a low boil until soft, about 5 minutes. Drain. Put the dried chiles into a blender or food processor with the fresh chiles; grind into a puree. Transfer to a bowl and set aside.

3. Grind the galangal, candlenuts, sliced lemongrass, shallots, and garlic to a smooth paste in a blender or food processor. Add a tablespoon or more of water if needed to facilitate the blending. Heat the oil in a wok or saucepan. When hot, carefully add the chile puree and fry, stirring continuously, until the oil takes on a reddish hue, about 1 minute. Add the ground mixture and fry, stirring frequently, until it combines completely with the oil. Continue frying and stirring until the *rempah* is creamy thick and fragrant, about 8 to 10 minutes. When reddish oil seeps out it is done. Add the remaining lemongrass, coconut milk, sugar, salt, and grated coconut; simmer

for 2 minutes. Add the chicken and simmer, uncovered, until the chicken is tender and is coated with the thick sauce, about 20 to 30 minutes. When oil seeps out of the sauce, the dish is done. Serve with rice. If you wish, let the chicken cool then refrigerate it; simply reheat to serve.

AYAM KAPITAN

Sweet and Lemony Chicken Thighs
(*Malay*)

Traditionally this dish is made with chicken parts; this version uses boned thighs. They are braised in a mildly spicy curry sauce with a refreshing sweet and lemony accent. If you prefer not to deep-fry the chicken in the initial cooking step, you may pan-fry it in a thin layer of oil.

Serves 6

8 chicken thighs
Vegetable oil for deep-frying

REMPAH
5 candlenuts, soaked in water for 10 minutes, or skinless almonds
5 stalks fresh lemongrass, trimmed and sliced
8 shallots (walnut-size) or 2 medium onions, peeled and sliced
12 cloves garlic, peeled and sliced
1½-inch chunk fresh ginger, peeled and sliced
8 red jalapeño chiles, stems removed
½ cup vegetable oil

✿

1 can (13½ ounces) unsweetened coconut milk
2 teaspoons salt
5 tablespoons sugar
½ cup water
Juice of 3 lemons
1 onion, cut into ¾-inch chunks

1. Put the thighs skin side down on a cutting board. With the tip of a knife cut along the length of the bone on both sides. Slip the knife tip under the bone to free the meat, then cut the meat away from the round ends of the bone. Remove the bone; pat the meat dry.

2. Preheat a wok; pour in 2 to 3 inches of oil and heat it to 365°F. Deep-fry the chicken a few pieces at a time until golden brown, about 5 minutes. Drain on paper towels.

3. To prepare the *rempah,* grind the candlenuts, lemongrass, shallots, garlic, ginger, and chiles to a smooth paste in a blender or food processor. Add a tablespoon or more of water if needed to facilitate the blending. Heat the ½ cup of oil in a wok or saucepan over medium heat. Add the ground mixture and fry, stirring frequently, until it is completely combined with the oil. Continue frying until the *rempah* is fragrant and has a light orange color and porridge-like consistency, about 8 minutes. It is ready when orange oil seeps out.

4. Add the coconut milk, salt, sugar, water, and lemon juice; simmer over medium heat, stirring, for 1 minute. Add the chicken and onion and continue cooking until the onion is tender and the chicken is heated through.

PATONG AYAM

Mild Coconut Chicken Curry

(*Nonya*)

Curry is one of the most frequently misused words in the culinary lexicon. Curry is not just a bottled spice (curry powder); it is a method of cooking and seasoning foods with a variety of complex spice blends. The finished dish can be "dry" (the liquids are reduced to a rich, spicy coating) or "wet" (the dish has a stew-like consistency). Curry flavors range from mild to medium to five-alarm hot.

Patong Ayam is a mild wet curry. Almost soupy, it makes a lovely dipping curry with Indian roti bread. Unlike pungent Indian curries flavored with cardamom, cloves, and cinnamon, Nonya-style curry chicken is temperate with subtle hints of lemongrass and galangal.

Serves 4 to 6

REMPAH
4 quarter-size slices fresh galangal, cut up (see Note, page 55)
4 candlenuts, soaked in water for 10 minutes, or skinless almonds
2 stalks fresh lemongrass, trimmed and sliced
8 shallots (walnut-size) or 2 medium onions, peeled and sliced
5 cloves garlic, peeled and sliced
1 slice *blachan* (dried shrimp paste), 1 inch square by 1/4 inch thick
1/3 cup vegetable oil
2 tablespoons Red Chile Paste (see page 39)
2 tablespoons Indian-style curry powder

✿

1 chicken (2 1/2 pounds), cut into parts
1 can (13 1/2 ounces) unsweetened coconut milk, plus 1 can water
1 large potato, peeled and cut into 1-inch chunks
2 teaspoons salt
1 tablespoon sugar

1. To prepare the *rempah*, grind the galangal, candlenuts, lemongrass, shallots, garlic, and *blachan* to a smooth paste in a blender or food processor. Add a tablespoon or more of water if needed to facilitate the blending. Heat the oil in a wok or saucepan over medium heat. Add the chile paste and fry for 2 minutes, stirring continuously, until the oil takes on a reddish hue. Add the ground mixture and fry, stirring frequently over low heat, until it is completely combined with the oil. Continue frying until the *rempah* is fragrant and has a dark mahogany-red color and porridge-like consistency, about 8 minutes. It is ready when reddish oil seeps out. Blend in the curry powder and simmer for 1 minute; set aside.

2. Bring a large pot of water to a boil. Add the chicken and bring to a second boil. Cook until scum rises to the surface, about 2 minutes. Remove the chicken.

3. In a large saucepan combine the coconut milk, water, chicken, and *rempah*. Bring to a boil, reduce the heat, and simmer for 30 minutes. Add the potato during the last 15 minutes of cooking. Season with salt and sugar. Serve warm.

MEAT DISHES

Nonya Spareribs (page 152)

STRAITS-STYLE BEEF IN A CRISP TARO BOWL

(*Straits Cafe*)

This recipe is a creation of the Straits Cafe. Sweet, juicy strips of quick wok-sauteed beef are beautifully presented in a crisp fried taro bowl. You will need two Chinese skimmers to form the bowl.

Serves 4 with other dishes

Vegetable oil for deep-frying
2 cups peeled, grated taro root
Pinch of salt
Pinch of flour
1 tablespoon chopped garlic
½ pound thinly sliced beef (flank steak or chuck)
3 tablespoons white wine
1 tablespoon sugar
1 tablespoon oyster sauce
1 teaspoon Asian sesame oil

1. Preheat a wok. Add 2 to 3 inches of oil and heat it to 365°F.

2. While the oil is heating, combine the grated taro root and salt in a large bowl. Add just enough flour to absorb the excess moisture. Dip two 6- to 7-inch-wide Chinese bamboo skimmers into the oil. Remove and drain. Line the bowl of one skimmer evenly with the taro root. Gently press it into shape by placing the other skimmer on top.

3. When the oil is hot, lower the two skimmers with the taro root pressed lightly between them into the oil. Deep-fry for a few seconds, then remove the top skimmer and continue frying until the taro "bowl" is golden brown, about 1 minute. Remove the taro bowl from the oil, gently loosen it from the skimmer, and drain it on paper towels. Set aside. Remove all but 2 tablespoons of the oil from the wok.

4. Heat the oil over medium heat. Add the garlic and saute until lightly brown. Raise the heat to high and toss in the beef; stir-fry to sear the beef, about 30 seconds to 1 minute. Quickly add the wine, sugar, oyster sauce, and sesame oil; stir-fry until the sauce turns into a glaze. Pour the beef into the taro bowl and serve hot.

KARI LEMBU

Indian-Style Red Curry Beef

(*Indian*)

This curry is a collage of spices, herbs, and seasonings. The sweet and pungent nip of cinnamon and herbal tones of cardamom, cloves, and curry leaves infuse the creamy coconut-milk sauce. Serve it as a side dish or as an entree accompanied by broccoli, cabbage, or cauliflower and rice.

Serves 4

1½ pounds beef chuck, cut into 1½-inch chunks

REMPAH
1-inch chunk fresh ginger, peeled and sliced
10 shallots (walnut-size) or 2 onions, peeled and halved
6 cloves garlic, peeled and sliced
1 stalk fresh lemongrass
¼ cup vegetable oil
3 tablespoons Red Chile Paste (see page 39)

✿

1 teaspoon cardamom pods
2 sticks cinnamon
½ teaspoon whole cloves
10 curry leaves (preferably fresh)
2 tablespoons Indian-style curry powder
½ can (6¾ ounces) unsweetened coconut milk, shaken well
1 teaspoon salt
1 teaspoon sugar
2 boiled potatoes, cut into 1-inch chunks

1. Parboil the beef for 1 minute (see *Kambing Kurma,* step 1, page 150). Drain and set aside.

2. Grind the ginger, shallots, and garlic to a smooth paste in a blender or food processor; set aside. Cut a 5-inch piece from the lemongrass stalk, starting at the root end; trim the piece and smash it with side of a cleaver. Set aside.

3. Heat the oil in a wok or saucepan over medium heat. Add the chile paste and fry, stirring continuously, until the oil takes on a reddish hue, about 2 minutes. Add the ground mixture and fry over low heat, stirring frequently, until it is completely combined with the oil, about 3 minutes. Continue frying until the *rempah* is fragrant and has a deep mahogany-red color and porridge-like consistency. When oil seeps out, it is cooked. Add the lemongrass, cardamom pods, cinnamon, cloves, curry leaves, and curry powder and fry lightly. Add the coconut milk, beef, salt, and sugar and simmer, stirring frequently, for 30 minutes or until the beef is tender. Add the potatoes during the last 5 minutes of cooking. Serve with rice.

BEEF TANDOORI

(*Straits Cafe*)

This signature dish created by Jenny Fong at the Straits Cafe is grilled, not cooked in a tandoori oven, but it nonetheless delivers the spirited flavors of Indian cooking. It tastes best when served with Indian Fry Bread (page 85) to dunk in the sauce. For a simple light meal, try serving it with steamed rice, blanched cauliflower, and stir-fried spinach. It also goes particularly well with a bowl of lentil soup on a cold winter night.

Serves 6 to 8

REMPAH
5 quarter-size slices fresh galangal, cut up (see Note, page 55)
3 stalks fresh lemongrass, trimmed and sliced
8 shallots (walnut-size) or 2 medium onions, peeled and halved
6 cloves garlic, peeled and halved
2-inch chunk fresh ginger, peeled and sliced
2 tablespoons Indian-style or Madras-style curry powder
1 teaspoon salt
4 teaspoons sugar
¾ cup unsweetened coconut milk (shake can well before measuring)

✿

1½ to 2 pounds flank steak
¼ cup vegetable oil
6 curry leaves
Sprigs of fresh coriander, for garnish

1. To prepare the *rempah*, grind the galangal, lemongrass, shallots, garlic, ginger, curry powder, salt, and sugar to a smooth paste in a blender or food processor. Add a tablespoon or more of water if needed to facilitate the blending. Mix in the coconut milk. Place the beef in a large shallow dish and pour the *rempah* over it; marinate for 1 hour. Meanwhile, prepare a hot charcoal fire.

2. Transfer the beef to a plate. Scrape off the *rempah* and reserve it with any *rempah* remaining in the dish. Set a wok over medium heat and add the oil, curry leaves, and *rempah*. Fry, stirring frequently, until the *rempah* is completely combined with the oil. Continue frying and stirring until the mixture is fragrant and has a porridge-like consistency, about 8 minutes. When oil seeps through the mixture, the sauce is done. Keep it warm.

3. Grill the beef over glowing hot coals, about 3 minutes on each side or to the desired doneness. Slice the meat diagonally against the grain. Spoon the sauce over the meat and garnish with sprigs of fresh coriander. Serve hot with Indian Fry Bread and Pickled Onion Rings (page 165).

KAMBING KURMA

Mild Lamb Curry
(*Malay*)

Cinnamon sticks and brown mustard seeds, popular spices of India, add a delicate pungency to this lamb curry. It serves well with steamed or stir-fried cauliflower, cabbage, and white rice.

Serves 6 to 8

2 pounds boned leg of lamb, cut into 1½-inch cubes

REMPAH
2-inch chunk ginger, peeled and sliced
12 shallots (walnut-size) or 2 large onions, peeled and sliced
10 cloves garlic, peeled and sliced
1 tablespoon white peppercorns
1 tablespoon cumin seeds
1 tablespoon fennel seeds
4 tablespoons coriander seeds
1 cup vegetable oil or ghee
½ teaspoon whole brown mustard seeds
3 sticks cinnamon
7 whole cloves
10 whole cardamom pods

✿

1 can (13½ ounces) coconut milk, shaken well
½ tablespoon salt
1 tablespoon sugar
½ cup water
5 tablespoons plain yogurt
4 red jalapeño chiles, halved lengthwise, stems and seeds removed
½ cup peas (optional)
½ cup cooked carrots, in ¼-inch dice (optional)
2 tomatoes, cut in quarters

1. Bring a large pot of water to a boil. Add the lamb and return to a boil. Boil for 1 minute or until scum rises to the surface. Remove the lamb; drain and set aside.

2. To prepare the *rempah*, grind the ginger, shallots, and garlic to a smooth paste in a blender or food processor. Add a tablespoon or more of water if needed to facilitate the blending; set aside. Grind the peppercorns, cumin, fennel, and coriander to a fine powder in a spice mill; set aside.

3. Set a wok over medium heat. Add the oil. When hot, carefully add the shallot mixture and

fry for a few minutes, but do not brown. Add the mustard seeds, cinnamon, cloves, and cardamom. Fry, stirring frequently, until the shallot mixture is completely combined with the oil. Continue frying and stirring until the mixture is creamy, thick, and fragrant, about 15 minutes. When oil seeps out, the *rempah* is cooked. Stir in the ground spices, coconut milk, salt, and sugar.

4. Add the parboiled lamb and water (or just enough water to keep the meat covered). Cook at a lively simmer, uncovered, for 20 minutes. Add the yogurt, red chiles, peas, carrots, and tomatoes. Cook for 10 minutes longer or until the lamb is tender. Serve with Nasi Kunyit (turmeric rice, page 84).

NONYA SPARERIBS

(*Nonya*)

Traditionally, Cantonese cooks braise spareribs in a fermented soybean sauce that is dark brown in color and rich in flavor. Southeast Asian cooks favor a milder yellow fermented bean sauce, *tau cheo,* which is the main seasoning in this Nonya-style sparerib recipe. Here it is augmented with soy sauce and fresh ginger, both very Chinese ingredients, and such characteristic Malay ingredients as lemongrass, vinegar, shallots, and chiles. This dish may be served as an appetizer.

Serves 4 with other dishes

1½ pounds pork spareribs, cut into cubes (see Note)
10 shallots (walnut-size) or 2 large onions, peeled and sliced
1-inch chunk ginger, peeled and sliced
8 cloves garlic, peeled and sliced
8 fresh red serrano chiles, stems removed, sliced
¼ cup vegetable oil
1 tablespoon *tau cheo* (yellow bean sauce), chopped
4 stalks fresh lemongrass, trimmed and slapped with a cleaver (optional)
3 tablespoons white vinegar
4 tablespoons sugar
2 cups water
1 tomato, cut into 1-inch cubes

1. Bring a large pot of water to a boil. Add the ribs and return the water to a boil. Boil for 1 minute or until scum rises to the surface. Remove the ribs and rinse with cold water; set aside.

2. Grind the shallots, ginger, garlic, and chiles to a smooth paste in a blender or food processor. Heat the oil in a wok or saucepan over medium heat. Add the ground mixture and bean sauce. Lightly saute the mixture, without browning it, for about 3 minutes. Add the lemongrass, vinegar, sugar, ribs, and water. Bring the mixture to a boil, reduce the heat, and cook at a gentle boil, uncovered, for 20 minutes. Stir occasionally until the sauce is reduced to a thick gravy. Fold in the tomato and cook 1 minute longer. Serve hot with rice.

NOTE: Have your butcher chop the ribs across the bones into 1¼-inch strips. When you get them home, cut between the ribs to make cubes.

NONYA DAGING RENDANG

Beef in Spicy Coconut-Lime Sauce
(*Nonya*)

The French cook uses cream to thicken sauces; the Southeast Asian cook prefers coconut milk. In this dish beef cubes are simmered in coconut milk until it is reduced to a thick gravy. Cooking with coconut milk can be tricky. For most vegetable dishes, it is cooked only until smooth and delicate; in meat dishes such as this one, slow simmering develops a thicker consistency and richer flavor. It is most important not to cover the pot during cooking and to stir frequently to prevent the coconut milk from curdling.

Much of the flavor of this dish is derived from kaffir lime leaves. If they are not available, use lime zest (the colored outer skin). Nonya Sweet-Sour Pineapple Pickles (page 163) or other fruit is a perfect accompaniment to the rich, spicy flavor of this dish.

Serves 4

1¼ pounds beef chuck, cut into 1¼-inch chunks
1-inch chunk fresh ginger, peeled and finely minced

REMPAH
1-inch chunk fresh galangal, sliced (see Note, page 55)
5 candlenuts, soaked in water for 10 minutes, or skinless almonds
3 stalks fresh lemongrass, trimmed and sliced
6 shallots (walnut-size) or 1½ onions, peeled and halved
5 cloves garlic, peeled and halved
¼ cup vegetable oil
2 tablespoons Red Chile Paste (see page 39)

✿

6 kaffir lime leaves or zest of 1 lime
½ can (6¾ ounces) unsweetened coconut milk, shaken well
Juice of ½ lemon
4 teaspoons sugar
1½ teaspoons salt
½ cup water

1. Toss the beef and ginger together in a bowl; set aside.

2. To prepare the *rempah,* grind the galangal, candlenuts, lemongrass, shallots, and garlic to a smooth paste in a blender or food processor. Add a tablespoon or more of water if needed to facilitate the blending. Heat the oil in a wok or saucepan over medium heat. Add the chile paste and fry, stirring continuously, until the oil takes on a reddish hue, about 2 minutes. Reduce the heat to low, add the ground mixture, and fry, stirring frequently, until it is completely combined

with the oil, about 3 minutes. Continue frying until the *rempah* has a rich, deep mahogany color and a porridge-like consistency, about 8 minutes. It is ready when reddish oil seeps out.

3. Split the lime leaves in half lengthwise, tear off and discard the spines, and cut the leaves into fine slivers. Add the coconut milk, beef chunks, lime leaves, lemon juice, sugar, salt, and water to the *rempah*. Simmer uncovered, stirring frequently, until the beef is tender and the sauce thickens, about 30 to 40 minutes. Serve with rice.

SAUCES AND GARNISHES

Satay Sauce
Sesame-Soy Dipping Sauce
Gingered Oil Dipping Sauce
Chile-Ginger Sambal
Sambal Blachan
Sweet Chile Sauce
Sweet-Sour Pineapple Pickles (*Puchuri Nanas*)
Pickled Vegetable Salad (*Achar*)
Pickled Onion Rings
Crisp Shallot Flakes (*Bawang Goreng*)
Fried Tofu Cubes
Potato Fritters (*Perkedel*)
Krupuk

Center: Chile-Ginger Sambal. Clockwise from top: Pickled Onion Rings, Achar, Sambal Blachan, *Satay Sauce,* Bawang Goreng, *Sweet Chile Sauce, Red Chile Paste*

SATAY SAUCE
(*Malay*)

Satay sauces seem to be universally loved, particularly by the Western palate. The original satay and satay peanut sauces come from Indonesia, as do many variations and interpretations. The neighboring countries of Malaysia and Thailand adopted this Indonesian style of cooking and created their own versions as well. This Malay-style satay sauce is also very good with blanched vegetables. Extra sauce may be frozen for future use.

Makes about 3½ cups

REMPAH
5 quarter-size slices fresh galangal, cut up (see Note, page 55)
5 candlenuts, soaked in water for 10 minutes, or skinless almonds
5 stalks fresh lemongrass, trimmed and sliced
10 shallots (walnut-size) or 2 onions, peeled and sliced
6 cloves garlic, peeled and sliced
1 teaspoon turmeric powder
1 cup vegetable oil
3 tablespoons Red Chile Paste (see page 39)

✿

1 can (13½ ounces) coconut milk, shaken well
½ cup tamarind water (see page 41)
5 tablespoons sugar
1½ teaspoons salt
2 cups ground roasted peanuts

1. To prepare the *rempah*, grind the galangal, candlenuts, lemongrass, shallots, garlic, and turmeric to a smooth paste in a blender or food processor. Add a tablespoon or more of water if needed to facilitate the blending. Heat a wok over low heat. Add the oil and chile paste and fry, stirring frequently, until the oil takes on a reddish hue, about 2 minutes. Add the ground mixture and fry, stirring frequently, until it is completely combined with the oil. Continue frying and stirring until the *rempah* is fragrant and has a porridge-like consistency, about 10 minutes. When reddish oil seeps out, it is done.

2. Add the coconut milk, tamarind water, sugar, salt, and peanuts. Simmer over low heat until oil separates from the sauce, about 10 minutes. Serve at room temperature with Satay (page 60).

SESAME-SOY DIPPING SAUCE
(*Chinese*)

This sauce is served with Hainanese Chicken Rice (page 136). The dark soy sauce, which comes from Thailand, is slightly sweeter and richer than Chinese-style dark soy sauce. It is more pleasing to the Singaporean palate.

Makes ¼ cup

2 tablespoons Asian sesame oil
2 tablespoons dark soy sauce (Kwong Hung Seng brand)

Mix the oil and soy sauce together thoroughly. Pour into dipping saucers.

GINGERED OIL DIPPING SAUCE
(*Chinese*)

Serve this dipping sauce with Hainanese Chicken Rice (page 136) or other poached chicken dishes.

Makes ¼ cup

1 tablespoon grated or finely minced peeled fresh ginger
1 teaspoon salt
3 tablespoons vegetable oil

Mix the ginger and salt in a heatproof bowl. Slowly heat the oil in a saucepan until it is hot but not smoking. Test the oil by slowly pouring a small amount over the ginger-salt mixture. If it does not sizzle, stop, return the saucepan to the stove, and continue heating the oil until it is hot enough to sizzle on contact with the ginger. Serve in dipping saucers.

CHILE-GINGER SAMBAL

(*Chinese—Hainanese*)

Sambals, chile-based dipping sauces, are used frequently as table condiments in Malaysia, Indonesia, and Singapore. There are likely to be many small flat dishes of different sambals at any given meal. For Chicken Rice (page 136) this sambal is a must, but it certainly is delicious with other dishes, too.

Makes about 1¼ cups

½ small lime
10 cloves garlic, peeled
4 1-inch chunks fresh ginger, peeled and sliced
12 fresh red serrano chiles
¼ cup rendered chicken fat or vegetable oil
3 tablespoons sugar
½ cup white vinegar

1. Rinse the lime before cutting it. Cut the lime half into wedges (leave the skin on). Puree the wedges in a blender or food processor with the garlic, ginger, and chiles.

2. Heat the fat in a saucepan over medium-low heat. Add the puree and cook for 5 minutes. Remove the pan from the heat and stir in the sugar and vinegar. Put about 1 tablespoon of sambal in a dipping saucer for each diner.

SAMBAL BLACHAN
(*Malay*)

This table condiment is served throughout Singapore and Malaysia. It may be an acquired taste; however, once that bridge has been crossed, it will open a vast new world of culinary enjoyment. To prevent the "aroma" of toasting *blachan* from lingering throughout the house, wrap it in a piece of foil before toasting. Use *Sambal Blachan* sparingly, about ½ teaspoon per person.

Makes about ¼ cup

1 slice *blachan* (dried shrimp paste), 1 inch square by ¼ inch thick
6 fresh red serrano or seeded jalapeño chiles
Pinch of salt
1 lime leaf, spine removed
¼ teaspoon sugar
1 teaspoon fresh lime juice

Toast the *blachan* for 1 minute on each side in a dry skillet over medium heat. Grind it with the chiles, salt, lime leaf, and sugar in a mortar or spice grinder. Blend the ingredients thoroughly and stir in the lime juice. Transfer to dipping saucers.

SWEET CHILE SAUCE

(*Nonya*)

This dipping sauce accompanies Samosas (page 52) and can also be served with Hainanese Chicken Rice (page 136). Store extra sauce in the refrigerator.

Makes about 1 cup

5 cloves garlic
2-inch chunk ginger, peeled and sliced
3 to 5 red jalapeño chiles, or to taste
2 tablespoons vegetable oil
½ cup sugar
1 teaspoon salt
1 cup vinegar

Finely chop the garlic, ginger, and chiles in a blender. Warm the oil in a saucepan. Add the chopped mixture, sugar, salt, and vinegar and simmer for a few minutes, until the sauce thickens. Cool before serving.

PUCHURI NANAS
Sweet-Sour Pineapple Pickles
(*Nonya*)

In a Singaporean meal various side dishes, condiments, chutneys, sambals, and pickles are served to complement the highly seasoned main courses. These pineapple pickles are perfect for balancing the spiciness of chile- or curry-based entrees. They are also good for practicing eating with your fingers, Singapore-style.

Serves 8 as a side dish

1 fresh pineapple

REMPAH
4 candlenuts, soaked in water for 10 minutes, or skinless almonds
2 stalks fresh lemongrass, trimmed and sliced
5 cloves garlic, peeled and sliced
1 onion, cut into chunks
⅓ cup vegetable oil
2 sticks cinnamon
5 cloves
2 tablespoons Red Chile Paste (see page 39)

✿

½ teaspoon salt
3 tablespoons sugar
3 tablespoons white vinegar

1. Slice off and discard both ends of the pineapple. Cut off the skin and cut the pineapple in half vertically. Cut each half crosswise into ½-inch-thick slices; set aside.

2. To prepare the *rempah*, grind the candlenuts, lemongrass, garlic, and onion to a smooth paste in a blender or mini-food processor. Add a tablespoon or more of water if needed to facilitate the blending. Heat the oil in a wok or saucepan. Add the cinnamon sticks, cloves, and chile paste and fry, stirring continuously, until the oil takes on a reddish hue, about 2 minutes. Add the ground mixture and fry over low heat, stirring frequently, until it is completely combined with the oil. Continue frying and stirring until the *rempah* is fragrant and has a deep mahogany color and porridge-like consistency, about 8 minutes. It is ready when oil seeps out.

3. Stir in the salt, sugar, and vinegar and cook until the sugar dissolves. Fold in the pineapple slices while hot. Transfer the mixture to a glass bowl and let it sit for 10 minutes or longer. Serve at room temperature.

ACHAR
Pickled Vegetable Salad
(*Nonya*)

Achar is an Indonesian-Malaysian pickled vegetable relish. Its sweet, sour, and spicy flavor refreshes the palate and enhances the taste of curries and grilled dishes. Other vegetables such as green beans, red and green bell peppers, and cabbage may be added or substituted, but remember to have a contrast of colors and textures. Traditionally for Nonya-style *achar* the vegetables are sun-dried for a day to remove moisture, then boiled in vinegar; the drying step is not necessary for this recipe.

Makes about 2 cups

1 cucumber
1 carrot
¼ head cauliflower

REMPAH
2 quarter-size slices fresh galangal, cut up (see Note, page 55)
2 candlenuts, soaked in water for 10 minutes, or skinless almonds
2 stalks fresh lemongrass, trimmed and sliced
8 shallots (walnut-size) or 2 medium onions, peeled and sliced
3 cloves garlic, peeled and sliced
1 tablespoon dried shrimp, rinsed with water and drained
1 teaspoon turmeric powder
¼ cup vegetable oil
2 tablespoons Red Chile Paste (see page 39)

✿

½ cup white vinegar
4 tablespoons sugar
3 tablespoons ground roasted peanuts
Toasted sesame seeds, for garnish

1. Cut the unpeeled cucumber in half lengthwise; remove the seeds. Cut the cucumber into 2½-inch-long by ¼-inch-wide sticks. Peel the carrot and cut it into the same size sticks. Trim the cauliflower and break it into bite-size florets. Set aside.

2. To prepare the *rempah*, grind the galangal, candlenuts, lemongrass, shallots, garlic, dried shrimp, and turmeric to a smooth paste in a blender or food processor. Add a tablespoon or more of water if needed to facilitate the blending. Heat the oil in a wok or saucepan over low heat. Add the chile paste and fry, stirring continuously, until the oil takes on a reddish hue, about 2 minutes. Add the ground mixture and fry, stirring frequently, until the *rempah* is fragrant and has a rich mahogany-red color and porridge-like consistency, about 8 minutes. It is ready when reddish oil seeps out.

3. Raise the heat to medium and add the vegetables, vinegar, sugar, and peanuts. Stir-fry until the vegetables are tender but crisp, about 5 minutes. Cool. Transfer the mixture to a jar. Let it sit for at least 3 hours to pickle. Cover and refrigerate. *Achar* will keep up to 2 weeks. Serve cold or at room temperature, garnished with sesame seeds.

PICKLED ONION RINGS

(Straits Cafe)

At the Straits Cafe these sweet and sour pickled onions are served with the house specialty, Beef Tandoori (page 148), and with *Murtabak* (meat-filled Indian bread, page 87). They are easy to prepare, store well for several days, and are equally delicious with other dishes.

Makes about 1½ cups

1 large red onion
½ teaspoon salt
¼ cup sugar
½ cup white vinegar

Peel the onion and cut it crosswise into very thin slices (about ⅛ inch). Toss the slices with the salt in a bowl and let them sit for 5 minutes. Stir the sugar and vinegar together in another bowl until the sugar dissolves. Remove the onion slices from their bowl and gently squeeze out the juices. Add the onions to the vinegar-sugar mixture and set aside for 2 hours or longer. The onions will keep in a covered bowl for about a week. Drain before serving.

BAWANG GORENG

Crisp Shallot Flakes
(*Indonesian/Malay*)

Crisp, tasty fried onions sprinkled over a dish add a burst of flavor to noodles, salads, soups, main courses, and even desserts. Commercially prepared fried shallot or onion flakes are available in Asian markets but, as usual, the best are homemade.

Makes about ½ cup

8 large shallots
Vegetable oil for deep-frying

Peel the shallots. Using a small sharp knife, slice them crosswise as thinly and evenly as possible. Fill a saucepan or wok no more than half full with oil (there must be enough oil for the shallots to float). Heat the oil to 300°F. Add the shallots and deep-fry slowly for 3 to 5 minutes or until they are golden brown and crisp. They should be completely dry with no remaining moisture. Drain on paper towels. When cool, store the shallot flakes in an airtight container. They should keep for several weeks.

FRIED TOFU CUBES

(*Chinese*)

Fried tofu (bean curd) cubes are added to stewed and braised dishes and to stir-fried vegetable entrees. They are also indispensable as a tasty garnish and can be stuffed and served as an appetizer. Ready-made fried tofu cubes are available in Asian markets in the refrigerated section, but they are easy to make yourself. Use the fresh firm bean curd found in American supermarkets.

Makes 1 pound

1 pound fresh firm tofu
Vegetable oil for deep-frying

Cut the bean curd into 1-inch cubes; blot them dry thoroughly. Preheat a wok, saucepan, or deep-fryer. Add 2 to 3 inches of oil and heat it to 365°F. Deep-fry a few cubes at a time until golden brown, about 3 to 4 minutes. Drain on paper towels. Store in a plastic bag in the refrigerator for up to 1 week.

POTATO PERKEDEL

Potato Fritters
(*Indonesian*)

There are two versions of these potato fritters, one made from mashed boiled potatoes and the other from mashed fried potatoes. We tested both and both were delicious, but we preferred the boiled version. Serve these fritters as a side dish or add a few to each serving of *Soto Ayam* (page 64), the wonderful chicken soup of Indonesia.

Makes about 8

2 russet potatoes, boiled and cooled
½ green onion, minced
¼ teaspoon salt
¼ teaspoon white pepper
1 egg, beaten
Vegetable oil for deep-frying

1. Mash the potatoes. Mix in the green onion, salt, and pepper. Roll the mixture into balls about the size of golf balls, then flatten them into 1½-inch patties; set aside.

2. Fill a wok or saucepan no more than half full with oil; heat the oil to 365°F. Dip the potato patties into the beaten egg. Gently lower them into the hot oil and deep-fry for 3 minutes or until golden brown. Serve hot or at room temperature.

KRUPUK
(*Indonesian*)

In Indonesia chips are called *krupuk*. The best-known type is made from shrimp. They are served as a snack, as a bread-like accompaniment to a meal, or as a garnish. Dried Indonesian *krupuk* chips are available in Southeast Asian markets. They may contain fish, rice, or nuts mixed with tapioca flour, eggs, and salt. The mixture is worked into a roll, steamed, sliced, and left to dry in the sun. When you drop the dehydrated flakes into hot oil, they will triple in size and become crispy. Some chips are so large you can use them as a plate. Chinese shrimp chips are made with more flour; they are thinner and milder-tasting, and go well with delicate dishes like *Yu Sang* (page 55). Fry only what you need for garnishing or snacking.

Vegetable oil for deep-frying
Dried *krupuk* chips

Preheat a wok, saucepan, or deep-fryer. Add 2 to 3 inches of oil and heat it to 365°F. Add a few chips and deep-fry for a few seconds until they expand. (If they do not expand immediately, the oil is not hot enough.) Remove the chips and drain on paper towels.

INDEX

Italic numbers indicate photos.

Metric Conversion Table

Follow this chart to convert the measurements in this book to their approximate metric equivalents. The metric amounts have been rounded; the slight variations in the conversion rate will not significantly change the recipes.

Liquid and Dry Volume	**Metric Equivalent**
1 teaspoon	5 ml
1 tablespoon (3 teaspoons)	15 ml
1/4 cup	60 ml
1/3 cup	80 ml
1/2 cup	125 ml
1 cup	250 ml
Weight	
1 ounce	28 grams
1/4 pound	113 grams
1/2 pound	225 grams
1 pound	450 grams
Linear	
1 inch	2.5 cm

Temperature

°Fahrenheit	°Celsius
155	70
165	75
185	85
200	95
275	135
300	150
325	160
350	175
375	190
400	205
450	230

Other Helpful Conversion Factors

Sugar, Rice, Flour	1 teaspoon = 10 grams
	1 cup = 220 grams
Cornstarch, Salt	1 teaspoon = 5 grams
	1 tablespoon = 15 grams

ABOUT THE AUTHORS

CHRIS YEO opened the Straits Cafe in San Francisco in 1987. When the restaurant first opened, his mother came from Singapore to cook and his sister and brothers waited on tables. Today the restaurant, in its second, larger location, is well established among Bay Area lovers of authentic Asian food. Its chef, Jenny Fong, is a Nonya cook from Malaysia. Yeo himself holds a degree from Singapore's Hotel & Catering School and worked for two years at the famous Mandarin Hotel in Singapore. His exacting standards and insistence on authenticity are the cornerstones on which his restaurant's outstanding reputation is built.

JOYCE JUE, a San Francisco native, is an internationally respected authority on Asian food and a popular cooking teacher. She regularly leads culinary tours of Hong Kong, Thailand, and Singapore. Her cookbook *Asian Appetizers* was pubished in 1991. She writes a biweekly column for the San Francisco *Chronicle* as well as magazine articles on Asian food.

OTHER COOKBOOKS AVAILABLE FROM HARLOW & RATNER

EVERYBODY'S WOKKING by Martin Yan
Companion book to the ever-popular public television series "Yan Can Cook." A 176-page quality paperback with 35 pages of stunning color photos. Everybody's favorite Chinese cook, Martin Yan makes healthful Chinese cooking simple and fun.

THE WELL-SEASONED WOK by Martin Yan
In this book and the companion 1993 "Yan Can Cook" public television series, Martin Yan explores more Chinese and Southeast Asian cooking and introduces an assortment of his own East-West dishes. Quality paperback, 192 pages including 31 full-page color photos.

MORE VEGETABLES, PLEASE: DELICIOUS VEGETABLE SIDE DISHES FOR EVERYDAY MEALS by Janet Fletcher
All the home cook needs to know to serve a tasty, nutritious vegetable as part of dinner every day. Includes 34 easy-to-cook vegetables and more than 200 ways to serve them, plus guides to buying, storing, cleaning, and cutting each vegetable. Quality paperback, 228 pages including 32 full-page color photos.

ASIAN APPETIZERS: EASY, EXOTIC FIRST COURSES TO DRESS UP ANY MEAL by Joyce Jue
More than 60 easy-to-prepare dishes that fit nicely into Western menus. The recipes are drawn from China, Thailand, Korea, Japan, Vietnam, Singapore, Indonesia, and the Philippines. Quality paperback, 132 pages including 30 full-page color photos.

Jay Harlow's BEER CUISINE: A COOKBOOK FOR BEER LOVERS
Much of the world's best food goes very, very well with beer. This exuberant collection offers 78 recipes ranging from snacks and nibbles to elegant dinners for company. A few recipes use beer as an ingredient. Includes a summary of beer history and a guide to styles of beer. Quality paperback, 132 pages, including 30 full-page color photos.

HARLOW & RATNER was founded in 1990 to publish high quality cookbooks that are as authoritative and useful as they are beautiful. All of the authors published under the Astolat Books imprint are accomplished professional cooks and cooking teachers. Recipes are true to their ethnic origins and easy to reproduce in the average home kitchen. Astolat Books are for anyone who loves to cook and wants to learn from the best.